EMPOWERED
CREATIVITY

PARTNERING WITH
GOD TO PRODUCE
THE MIRACULOUS

ART THOMAS

SUPERNATURAL TRUTH PRODUCTIONS, LLC
Practical Training for Spirit-Filled Living
www.SupernaturalTruth.com

Empowered Creativity: Partnering with God to Produce the Miraculous
By Art Thomas

© Copyright 2022, Art Thomas.

ISBN: 978-0-9988171-9-4

ENDORSEMENTS

Whether or not you see yourself as creative, read this book. I have many strengths, but being artistic is nowhere near the top of the list. I can barely print my name, never mind draw. I'm musically challenged. I dreaded art class growing up. But every chapter of this book spoke to me and made me feel more alive. Why? Because it is filled with biblical truths and practical examples about our amazing Creator God and how he wants to bring his life in and through us. If, like me, you enjoy being inspired to function more in sync with how you were created, you won't be able to put down this book.

~ Tom Ruotolo
Founder, City Quake

The name Art Thomas is synonymous with a passion for the Holy Spirit and a strong creative gifting. The book you hold in your hand is the melding of these two worlds, proven in the fire of personal experience. God has a stronger anointing and a more profound creative gifting for you!

~ Tim Enloe
Author and Conference Speaker

The church has, for ages, notoriously kept God in boxes of religious limitation. While many have known Christianity as merely church attendance and Bible study, Art reveals a virtually untapped frontier of creative revelation and adventure that Christ has been begging his people to explore. Surely, it is of no coincidence he would call a man named "Art" to unpack it! This book not only educates; it inspires. Whether you are a painter, musician, doctor, businessman or housewife, God's creative miracles are waiting to be revealed through you.

~ Josh Adkins
The Loft Church
Author of *Heaven Here*

In *Empowered Creativity,* Art Thomas lays out a simple yet convincing explanation for our expression of the divine in everything we set out to do, tying it in biblically with who we now have become through our rebirth. Our Father has always been a Creator, and now, through his Spirit, he lives inside of us.

~ Shawn Hurley
Happy Hands Ministries

I've known Art Thomas for almost a decade now. When we first met, he let me watch the documentary *Paid in Full,* which he had just finished producing. We hit it off and have been friends ever since.

I've seen him produce a lot of fruit in various art forms for the kingdom of God and watched him attempt various new ideas I'd never heard of or thought of, particularly in the book publishing realm.

But that's not my point. Art has always been a trailblazer and willing to take risks or implement ideas from "off the beaten path." It's no surprise to me he's come up with this particular book, in a category all its own, just as I've come to expect from Art.

Going through the pages of *Empowered Creativity,* I can't help but wonder what has taken so long and why this particular book is only coming to fruition now. Even though all things happen in God's time, I can't help but also think, *It's about time!*

~ Steve Bremner
Author and Kingdom Writing Coach

Art Thomas is one of the most creative men that I know. In the years we've been colleagues, I have watched him launch several flourishing enterprises—design, publishing, filmmaking, discipleship, and the application of spiritual gifts. So, when I found out he penned a book on *Empowered Creativity,* I knew I had to have it. Going through these pages reconfirmed my friend's brilliance. Art is not only innovative in mind but also in execution. I'm not aware of any other books on this topic. So it looks like Art just broke open a whole new publishing category. I'm not surprised.

~ J.D. King
Author of *Shift: Leading in Transition*
and *Regeneration: A Complete History of Healing
in the Christian Church* (3 volumes)

Art Thomas is one of the most qualified people I can think of to write this book. As an author, musician, and filmmaker, Art leans into the prophetic voice of the Holy Spirit with every endeavor. His creative works always carry the empowering presence of the Holy Spirit. I know this book will bless you.

~ JonMark Baker
Author of *The Adventure of Saying Yes*
Spiritual Life Director, Roots Church

In the beginning, God created. Then, he immediately began releasing to humankind artistic, innovative, and strategic expressions of creativity to continuously reveal himself. Much of creativity has been seemingly siphoned off by the world—sometimes even rejected by the church. Art Thomas's *Empowered Creativity* exposes what has gone missing and inspires reconnection to the multifaceted dynamic of creativity; when the natural and the supernatural realms collide and when talents and spiritual gifts connect, manifestations of creativity become kingdom-advancing spectacular!

~ Quinn Schipper
Author of *Trading Faces, The Language of Forgiveness,*
and *The View – The Voice of God*

Art Thomas is creative to his core, and he truly desires to equip the body of Christ. This pairing makes him the right person to teach on inspiration and how it is truly best expressed in submission and partnership with the Holy Spirit. He embodies the Scripture: "Let us think of ways to motivate one another to acts of love and good works" (Hebrews 10:24 NLT).

Empowered Creativity is an invitation to dream with the Lord and partner with his unending imagination—not for the sake of your own gain but to discover all God has for your life, and to encounter the Source of creativity himself. I pray you are challenged and transformed to look more like Jesus than you did before.

~ James Loruss
Composer, Filmmaker, and Author
Worship/Arts Pastor, Northville Christian Assembly

Empowered Creativity contains powerful concepts that can change the way believers think about creativity. Art Thomas reveals how God will engage your creativity to bring heavenly realities to earth, to fight spiritual battles, to love people, and so much more.

~ J. Scott McElroy
Author of *Finding Divine Inspiration* and *Creative Church Handbook*
Founder, New Renaissance Arts Movement

For decades, the loudest voice defining creativity has been secular culture, rather than Christian communities. Many believers have yet to understand and implement supernatural creativity. Art Thomas restores our perspectives of creativity by highlighting overlooked Scripture passages alongside compelling personal testimonies. Artistry is neither inconsequential nor merely entertaining. The creations of Christian artists and makers supernaturally depict heaven on earth.

In *Empowered Creativity,* Art wisely defines Biblical creativity as an activity for all the children of God. If you consider yourself to be among "the least of these" in your creative sensibilities, this book will ignite your belief that God can and will inspire your imagination.

~ Natalie K. Ziemba
Visual Art Director, United Adoration

I will now tell you and our young friend here about my method of communicating with the Infinite, for all truly inspired ideas come from God. Beethoven, who was my ideal, was well aware of this.

When I feel the urge, I begin by appealing directly to my Maker and I first ask Him the three most important questions pertaining to our life here in this world—whence, wherefore, whither?

Straightaway the ideas flow in upon me, directly from God, and not only do I see distinct themes in my mind's eye, but they are clothed in the right forms, harmonies and orchestration.

. . . Jesus was the world's supreme spiritual genius, and He was conscious of appropriating the only true source of power as no one else ever was.

. . . Jesus Himself was very explicit about this, in saying, "Ask and it shall be given you, seek and ye shall find; knock and it shall be opened unto you." There would not be so much good music paper wasted in fruitless attempts to compose if those great precepts were better understood.

—Johannes Brahms (1833–1897)

ACKNOWLEDGMENTS

I was born into a rather creative family.

My mom was constantly coming up with inventions when I was a kid—whether it was the wearable car she built for me out of a diaper box and suspenders or the three-dimensional fabric landscape she sewed together for me to play on with my plastic dinosaurs.

My dad had a Lionel train set that filled an entire room with four levels of tracks and a system of switches that could send a train all the way from the bottom to the top and back again. Still today, at eighty years old, he plays the organ and keyboards and is constantly dreaming up new projects to do.

My brother is a writer, poet, musician, and painter; my sister is a dancer and doll-maker; and my other sister sculpts and draws.

In short, I was plopped into the middle of the perfect environment for creativity to bud, blossom, and flourish, and for that, I thank God.

As much as my family atmosphere and genetics were in my favor, I know that my most effective creativity comes from another place. So while I do want to honor my earthly mom and dad for my creativity and for, in many ways, laying the foundations of this book, the greater glory must go to my heavenly Daddy. My parents were the vessels God used to bring together two very unique sets of DNA, gifting me my genetic predispositions. My parents were the vessels he used to raise me in a Christian home, to encourage me, to discipline me, and to create opportunities for me to become who he wants me to be. My parents receive the credit for being obedient to the Lord, but the Lord receives the credit for making me who I am.

From that perspective, I want to open this book by expressing how grateful I am to all those who have faithfully served God as his vessels to bring about transformation in me. First were my parents, then my siblings who encouraged my creativity, and then the many teachers who drew it out of me. I can't name everyone, but I would like to mention a few.

My wife, Robin, is a constant encouragement. She was calling me "Arthur the Author" before I even published my first book. She relentlessly prophesies destiny and purpose into my life to keep my focus on God's mission. Without her unwavering support and loving participation, I wouldn't be doing what I'm doing. Robin is a consistent helpmate who is always there to point me to God and give me the boost I need to stay on target with my calling.

In my first book, *The Word of Knowledge in Action*, I highlighted several pastors and authors who have all played a role in shaping my theology and ministry. But in the context of this book's topic, I simply want to highlight Pastor Dan Vander Velde.

When I went with him to plant Fowlerville Freedom Center, Pastor Dan inspired me to engage in the creativity of heaven. He challenged me to think outside the box in regard to how we do what we call church. We were constantly pushing the boundaries of what we knew as we followed the prompting of the Holy Spirit. Pastor Dan helped bring spiritual significance into my musical gifts by encouraging me to sing spontaneously, prophesy, and give our musicians room for improvised instrumentals when I led worship. We brought artwork and dance into the church worship setting. Our little church became a place where people could express themselves to God, and God was free to express himself back. I'm so grateful to Pastor Dan for opening my eyes to a whole new world of creativity in the church.

Before wrapping up, I want to give a special shout-out to my editor, Lisa Thompson. Her skills made an already great book even better (if I do say so myself). Lisa is a delight to work with, and she selflessly makes me look like a better author than I am.

Finally, I want to speak directly to all the people who are part of Roots Church—the church I serve today:

You have taken an incredible leap of faith, diving into a unique church that does things differently so we can reach the people no one else is reaching. Your passion for the lost, your zeal for miracles, and your love for Jesus and each other are all exemplary. I pray that this book inspires you to step out in all your gifts and talents to bring new, beautiful, and exciting expressions of Jesus into the earth.

TABLE OF CONTENTS

Foreword by Jeremiah Grube   3

Preface   7

Introduction   13

1)   Spirit-Empowered Creativity   21
2)   The Prophetic Potential of Creativity   39
3)   The Craftsmanship of God   51
4)   Creativity and World Transformation   69
5)   Natural Talents and Spiritual Gifts   87
6)   The Key to Powerful Creativity   101
7)   Overcoming the Assault against Creative People   119
8)   Creativity and Supernatural Power   129
9)   Creativity and Changing Spiritual Atmospheres   143
10)   Spending Time with the Creator   155
11)   Limitless, Love-Filled Creativity in Action   171
12)   Unleashing Empowered Creativity   183

Conclusion   205

About the Author   209

EMPOWERED CREATIVITY ~ Art Thomas

*G*od is not a one-dimensional God. Yes, he uses preachers, pastors, and evangelists on an everyday basis to advance his kingdom, but he also uses the creativity that he placed inside everyday Christians, which comes in various, beautiful forms to demonstrate the life-changing power of Jesus Christ on the planet.

Art Thomas has tapped into the very heart of God to simplistically unpack how vital creativity is to world transformation and paramount in reaching the lost for Christ. Not everyone will enter a church or attend a gospel crusade, but most people enjoy some form of music, art, poetry, reading, movies, etc.

I know the message of this book is true because I've witnessed it in action. I have seen countless miracles, healings, and salvations come from the very creative forms that God uses in his people today.

A number of years ago, I released a piano instrumental CD called *The Room*. The Lord challenged me to capture the very notes and melodies that he placed in my heart. Through a crazy set of miraculous circumstances, I was able to record a piano instrumental CD in Muscle Shoals, Alabama, with Hall of Fame guitarist Will McFarlane.

In preparing this foreword, Art asked me to share a few stories of what God has done with that album. Since it was released, I have received countless testimonies.

Schoolteachers played *The Room* in their classrooms. Students who had been misbehaving suddenly began to be respectful, kind, calm, and focused on their assignments.

Parents and grandparents who had autistic children and grandchildren played the CD while in the home. Numerous times, when the piano music began to play, the autistic kids shook less, had uplifted spirits, and became less and less agitated.

And recently, a pastor's eight-year-old son was suffering with night terrors and could not sleep through the night without waking up, screaming. This pastor, from Virginia Beach, Virginia, sent me a video testimony of how more than a year has passed of playing the CD every day, 24/7, in his son's bedroom; and in all that time, from the very first night, the boy has not had a single night terror.

God's creativity, flowing through us in ways that we could only imagine, is vital for advancing the life-changing power and healing of Jesus Christ!

Art does a brilliant job of driving home the importance of spending time with the Creator, using your creativity in a love-filled way, and emphasizing the influence that our creativity has on people and this planet. Do yourself a favor and spend some time reading, highlighting, and digesting Art's God-given inspiration in *Empowered Creativity*.

Jeremiah Grube

President of Lion of Judah Ministries
Former worship leader for Power and Love Ministries (Tom Ruotolo) and Lifestyle Christianity (Todd White), 2008–2018
Worship leader for City Quake, 2020–present

www.lionofjudahroar.com

EMPOWERED CREATIVITY ~ Art Thomas

PREFACE

*M*any of the scriptural discoveries and revelations found in this book came to me in 2010. At the time, I was transitioning from my role on staff at my previous church into my current role of traveling around the world to minister the gospel and equip believers for ministry. While I had already finished the initial manuscript for this book and had already signed a publishing contract, I felt in my spirit that I needed to wait a few years until the right time.

Little did I know what would transpire in the following few years of ministry. Along with a good friend, James Loruss, I produced and directed a feature-length film about physical healing. Since its release in 2014, *Paid in Full* has been shown hundreds of thousands of times to people on every continent. I was blessed to appear on Sid Roth's *It's Supernatural* and Daniel Kolenda's *Christ for All Nations* television programs. And then our movie aired multiple times around the world on GodTV.

We have received countless emails of amazing testimonies from people who were either healed while watching the movie, healed after practicing what they learned in the movie, or activated in healing ministry toward others, seeing God work miracles through their hands for the first time.

In 2017, my second movie, *Voice of God*, was released. This time, I paid translators to create subtitles, and a few of them reported to me that they wept through the entire translation process. When we premiered the film to a small crowd of friends and their guests, people were healed, set free, and had amazing encounters with God.

Over the years, I have written prophetic songs that God has used to minister to people in my church. I have continued to write books and articles as I sense the Lord's grace empowering me to minister through words on a page. I even painted my first prophetic painting in 2020, which proved to be a blessing to the widow to whom I gifted it.

The theories in my original manuscript are now being proven in the real world. My experiences of partnering with God through the creative process helped me to flesh out some parts of this book that were previously only concepts and observations. What you hold in your hands today is a book born out of biblical study and prayerful meditation, then sharpened through practical, personal experience.

This book is for every believer who wants to take his or her creativity to the next level. Whereas many other books have been written to help inspire creativity and encourage believers to use their imagination, the threefold focus of this book will primarily be to (1) educate you on the spiritual aspects of creativity, (2) show the miraculous results of faith when expressed through the creative process, and (3) equip you with practical insights on how to partner with God in designing and producing new creations that carry spiritual significance.

While I'm probably best known as a filmmaker, guest speaker, and author, you'll find that this is not a book about writing, speaking, or videography. I regularly engage in plenty of other creative expressions, including graphic design, web development, cooking, songwriting, musicianship, poetry, painting, and more. Whatever your preferred expression of creativity may be, you should be able to relate to the topics in this book. While some examples pertain to specific forms of creativity, this book is ultimately about the creative presence of Jesus in you and how to partner with him in producing physical objects that bear spiritual fruit.

This book presents a key passion of mine—that Christians would express Jesus through every medium and in every arena that is consistent with our faith. The world is already saturated with people expressing themselves, their cultures, their families, and their heritage. But we believers have a new "self" with a different culture, a different family, and a different heritage. Let's be different! Let's express the superior realities of heaven more than we express the inferior realities of earth.

Ultimately, all true creativity comes from God. He places a measure of it in every human being. Sometimes, that creativity is hindered and sometimes, it is fanned into flame, but it will always be limited for those who remain bound to this world and its desires. Instead, we must invite the Holy Spirit to set us and our creativity free so that we might express the limitless creativity of heaven.

God is the Creator by nature, and his Word tells us this:

> Through [God's glory and goodness] he has given us his very great and precious promises, so that through them *you may participate in the divine nature,* having escaped the corruption in the world caused by evil desires. (2 Peter 1:4, emphasis added)

Be encouraged to participate in God's divine creativity. It's better than anything you received from your genetics, the environment, or even all the practice in the world. Expressing God's creativity is expressing God himself.

As you read this book, I pray that you will encounter the Holy Spirit and be transformed more and more into the likeness of

Christ. Seek to express him, and you will find an endless supply of empowered creativity.

INTRODUCTION

*I*n August of 2014, Jim was given three months to live. At only sixty-nine-years-old, prostate cancer was winning.

As a long-time friend of our family, my parents sent him a copy of a movie I made with my friend James Loruss, *Paid in Full*. In September, with only two months left on his clock, Jim watched footage of miracles happening around the world and listened to about thirty people talk about the simplicity of healing ministry.

At some point in the middle of watching the film, the Holy Spirit spoke to Jim's heart: "Don't worry about the cancer. Go live your life."

Jim knew God had healed him. He soon returned to his doctor for further tests, and that's when the big shocker came. The doctor spoke the exact words the Holy Spirit had stirred in Jim: "Don't worry about the cancer. Go live your life."

Jim had been healed.

As I write this about eight years later, Jim is still doing great.

Was it the movie that healed my friend Jim? Of course not. But did God use that movie to bring healing to him? It certainly would appear so!

I can't tell you how many e-mails I have received from people who were healed while watching our movie. And I've received many more from people who put the message of the film into action and immediately started seeing results in healing ministry. Who would have thought that a human act of creativity would produce such supernatural results?

When my friend James first approached me in 2011 about making our movie, neither of us had any experience with filmmaking. We had no equipment, no money, no connections, and no idea what we were doing. But since I had already written the first draft of this book, I knew it was possible to partner with God in the creative process and see things come together.

We learned a lot along the way. When God enters our creative process, he doesn't take over and do everything himself. I'm sure God could have made a much better film than we did if he had made it himself. What he actually does is empower us— amplifying our natural abilities, inspiring new ideas, and backing up our work by producing a supernatural impact from it. There's no way James and I could—in our own strength—make a movie that heals cancer. That's not even within the realm of human possibility. But there's no question about whether God can place his own seal of approval on a project—especially if we will partner with him along the way.

God loves to partner with us in the creative process. Creativity is the first attribute of God we see in Scripture. The first verse of the entire Bible says, "In the beginning, God created …" It was no mistake that when God created mankind in his image, he created us with a capacity for creativity too. It's the family business!

Unfortunately, when mankind fell, our creativity fell with us. Rather than inventing creations God would want to empower, we began inventing new ways of doing evil. (See Romans 1:30.) When God sees the multiplication, amplification, or glorification of sin, he backs out of our creative process. We are left to create apart from God and in mere human strength—monuments to our own abilities. (See Genesis 11:1–9.) When God sees our pride expressed through human self-sufficiency, he opposes it. (See James 4:6.)

Not all creativity is empowered creativity. God uses his power to confirm truth. (See Mark 16:20.) When we produce creations purely out of our human flesh, we miss out on an incredible opportunity to partner with God.

Partnering with God in creativity means engaging in creativity the way he does it. When God created the earth, his Spirit was fully engaged in the process. (See Genesis 1:2.) If you're going to engage in creativity that looks like Father God, then your spirit must also be fully engaged. This requires that we be new creations. (See 2

Corinthians 5:17.) Until we surrender our lives to Jesus, our human spirits are dead. (See Ephesians 2:1–9.) But once we have entered into a relationship with him and been made alive by the Holy Spirit, we are awake and ready to engage in active partnership with God. This is where empowered creativity happens.

While God may be finished creating the earth, he never stopped being creative. Today, his greatest creative work happens every day as he makes people around the world into new creations. And we—as new creations—become carriers of that creativity. Just as our creativity fell when mankind fell, so was our creativity redeemed when we were redeemed. Christians have the capacity to express the sort of creativity that God wants to partner with, and that's what this book is all about.

Expressing empowered creativity requires that you embrace your new identity in Christ. He has made you righteous. (See 2 Corinthians 5:21.) You are one with him in spirit. (See 1 Corinthians 6:17.) Your sinful nature has been crucified, and you no longer live—Christ lives in you. (See Galatians 2:20.) As a result, your creativity is actually the creativity of Jesus being uniquely revealed through a new creation—someone who never previously existed but who bears the life and presence of Christ himself through the indwelling Holy Spirit.

Jesus wants you to live fully free from the trappings of your old nature and settle firmly into your new nature, which looks like him at its core. He wants to express his creativity through you as you engage your renewed mind and dream of new possibilities that have never existed before. It's your nature to think this way. And when you couple the creativity of your new nature with the mission of your new nature (making disciples, revealing God's kingdom, and destroying the devil's work), God pours himself into your work and partners with you to create what's far beyond your human ability.

I want to take you on a journey in which you discover how to diverge from the pride of mere human imagination and learn to express the insurmountable creativity of our God that flows from a transformed life.

As the body of Christ, we—the church—are the physical presence of Jesus in this world. Yes, Jesus exists in a complete human form at the right hand of the Father in heaven; but as far as his ministry in this world is concerned, the Holy Spirit has made each of us a living extension of him. (See 1 Corinthians 6:15.) Thus, it can be true of us that everything we do can be done in the name of Jesus. (See Colossians 3:17.)

Jesus is creative; and as his body, we express that creativity. The God who created the entire universe—things seen and things invisible—dwells within you. By studying his creativity, we come to know his ways and learn to express his heart more meaningfully.

Consider what the Bible says about our Lord's creativity:

> In the past God spoke to our ancestors through the prophets at many times and in various ways, but in these last days he has spoken to us by his Son, whom he

appointed heir of all things, and *through whom also he made the universe.* The Son is the radiance of God's glory and the exact representation of his being, sustaining all things by his powerful word. After he had provided purification for sins, he sat down at the right hand of the Majesty in heaven. (Hebrews 1:1–3, emphasis added)

Through him all things were made; without him nothing was made that has been made .... He was in the world, and though the world was made through him, the world did not recognize him. (John 1:3, 10)

The Son is the image of the invisible God, the firstborn over all creation. For in him all things were created: things in heaven and on earth, visible and invisible, whether thrones or powers or rulers or authorities; all things have been created through him and for him. He is before all things, and in him all things hold together. And he is the head of the body, the church; he is the beginning and the firstborn from among the dead, so that in everything he might have the supremacy. For God was pleased to have all his fullness dwell in him, and through him to reconcile to himself all things, whether things on earth or things in heaven, by making peace through his blood, shed on the cross. (Colossians 1:15–20)

Again, Jesus is creative. Notice in the last passage that right after describing Christ's creativity, Paul says, "And he is the head of the body, the church." Jesus's creative power is still at work today, and his preferred method of expression appears to be in and through his people!

My desire is to see the body of Christ expressing the creativity of Christ. While most of the world operates in the limited creativity of their fallen nature, the church—made alive in Christ—should be tapped into the infinite supply of God's own creative flow. Imagine the unending possibilities of expressing God's creativity through the Holy Spirit's power. We may not enjoy speaking a literal universe into existence like he did, but we do enjoy the privilege of carrying out and establishing his divine purposes for this universe in ways that bring glory to him.

Like Moses, you can sculpt a snake that cures those who look at it. Like Ezekiel, you can make a model that proclaims a prophetic word in a visual way. Or like James and me, you can make a movie that ministers healing and equips people to walk in power. The only limits exist when we drift into pride, mere human effort, or the old nature. But when Jesus lives through you, his Spirit will partner with your spirit, and the creative results will be unstoppable.

Some of this book is a prophetic call into new territories. As such, I fully admit that I don't have modern examples for every concept presented. Nevertheless, my prayer—and expectation—is that readers like you will apply the biblical examples to produce truly supernatural works of creativity.

Throughout this book, I will lay a foundation for this idea of empowered creativity. Not only will you discover how it works but how to put it into action and express God's creativity. We will also consider how to walk in the necessary spiritual freedom where true creativity can be expressed unhindered.

Creativity is a broad and diverse topic that ranges from the arts to business to ways of raising a family. Your particular expressions may be artistic in nature (painting, sculpting, dancing, singing, etc.), innovative in nature (inventing, planning, cooking, designing), or strategic in nature (business strategies, financial prowess, family management, marketing ingenuity, etc.). I'm not by any means an expert in every field or expression of creativity, so I won't be sharing tips and methods for specific skill-improvement. What I will do is reveal how to bring the boundless, supernatural creativity of God into your field of interest—whatever that may be.

In your hands is a guide to expressing the heart of God— allowing the Holy Spirit to breathe real spiritual life into otherwise empty hobbies and earthly talents. Again, I won't fill time teaching you how to sharpen your earthly skills—there are already plenty of books about that. On the contrary, we will now take a journey into the depths of God's infinite creativity and discover how to express it in this world through the presence of his Holy Spirit.

CHAPTER 1

SPIRIT-EMPOWERED CREATIVITY

When we harness the power of the redeemed imagination and
set our hearts on things above, heavenly things happen.
—Bob Hazlett

*T*he people awoke to a stomach-dropping explosion of thunder and the overwhelming drone of the loudest and longest trumpet blast they had ever heard. With trembling fingers, they pried open the cloth doors of their tents. A massive, black cloud swirled above and around the mountain by which they camped, flashing with lightning and crackling with thunder. The relentless trumpet blast continued to intensify.

Everyone assembled. Children covered their ears as their mothers gathered them to their sides. Men trembled. Animals widened their eyes, turning their backs to the storm while some tugged at the rocks and posts to which they were tied.

An old man pressed through the crowd, working his way toward the mountain. With his face to the wind and his staff in hand, he signaled for everyone to follow him. Slowly and cautiously, the people followed the old man toward the raging mountain and away from their camp.

The earth shook. Fire roared across the mountain, only occasionally visible through the thick smoke. Contrary to all logic, the people didn't flee the storm or the blazing mountain—they approached it. The old man led them right to the foot of the towering rock and gave strict orders not to move any further.

Moses called into the thick smoke, and God replied from the mountain to invite him to the top.[1]

There on Mount Sinai, God revealed to Moses a heavenly pattern so that he could return to his people and lead them in dynamic, powerful worship.

> They serve at a sanctuary that is a copy and shadow of what is in heaven. This is why Moses was warned when he was about to build the tabernacle: "See to it that you make everything according to the pattern shown you on the mountain." (Hebrews 8:5)

---

[1] Adapted from Exodus 19:16–20.

Moses received a front-row seat at a heavenly exhibition—seeing things that no other Israelite had the privilege to see. Yet even though it was Moses who had peered into the heavenly realm and understood the instructions, God saw fit to empower other people with the necessary gifts of creativity, artistry, sculpture, metalworking, design, and assembly to carry out the project.

> Then the Lord said to Moses, "See, I have chosen Bezalel son of Uri, the son of Hur, of the tribe of Judah, and I have filled him with the Spirit of God, with wisdom, with understanding, with knowledge and with all kinds of skills—to make artistic designs for work in gold, silver and bronze, to cut and set stones, to work in wood, and to engage in all kinds of crafts. Moreover, I have appointed Oholiab son of Ahisamak, of the tribe of Dan, to help him. Also I have given ability to all the skilled workers to make everything I have commanded you." (Exodus 31:1–6)

Moses may have seen the heavenly models and blueprints firsthand, but God gave other people the responsibility to carry out the work.

Interestingly, we don't see Moses micromanaging the project. We don't read about him saying, "Nope—that's not what I saw on the mountain." Rather, he allowed God's creative gifts in the people to flesh out the Father's revealed will. Throughout four full chapters in Exodus, the craftsmen of Israel worked hard building everything for the tabernacle. Only after everything was complete did Moses finally come to see what they produced.

> The Israelites had done all the work just as the Lord had commanded Moses. Moses inspected the work and saw that they had done it just as the Lord had commanded. So Moses blessed them. (Exodus 39:42–43)

Do you see what happened? God had so empowered the creativity and talent of the Israelites that all they needed from Moses were basic dimensions and materials. They had nothing but simple instructions and their own abilities and creativity. But they were so empowered by the Holy Spirit that when Moses came, he was able to essentially say, "Yes. That's exactly what I saw on the mountain. Well done."

Somehow, even with such rudimentary input, the craftsmen managed to construct copies of what Moses saw in heaven. We don't see any indication that they received divine revelation like Moses did. We simply see that God empowered their creativity. Moses gave them the basic guidelines and allowed their creativity to work out the details.

The result was the tabernacle and all its furnishings, where God would dwell with his people and reveal his glorious, powerful, awesome presence on earth. The Israelites' craftsmanship, artistry, and creativity became acts of obedience, worship, and spiritual warfare for their entire nation.

Bringing Heavenly Realities to Earth

When God empowers our creativity, we bring heavenly realities to earth. Sometimes we reveal creations that exist only in God's heart. Other times, we create things that give people a glimpse of what's in heaven. Still other times, we might create something that helps people encounter God and experience the heavenly realities themselves.

I made my first website back in 2002. I didn't know what I was doing, but the internet wasn't much to look at back then anyhow, so my cheesy site looked downright professional. Soon after, the new church I was helping plant needed a website, and I was tasked with the project. I didn't even know where to start, so I prayed.

During prayer, I had a vision of a huge library. I felt drawn to a particular shelf and saw a thick, leather-bound book with the name of our new church on the binding. Curious, I thumbed through the pages from back to front and found that most of the pages were blank. I found this to be an encouraging invitation to dream and create with the Lord in the days ahead.

Soon, the pages fell open to an image of a web page. It wasn't a drawing or a photo. The page was somehow digital, as though I were looking at the actual website. I watched the image scroll up and down, and the site navigated through a handful of pages. As I watched in this vision, I found myself understanding exactly what I was supposed to do to make the website. I closed the book, and the vision ended.

I immediately set to work on the website and made it in record time. It was a great-looking site too. That website served us well for the years I was part of that church and for years after.

The craftsmen of Israel may not have seen the "things in heaven" like Moses did, but they did—according to the author of Hebrews—manage to produce "a copy and a shadow" of those things. By engaging in the creative process, the Israelites brought heaven to earth.

Jesus reinforced this principle. Our Lord taught us to pray to the Father, "May your kingdom come and your will be done here on earth, just like your will is done in heaven" (Luke 11:2, paraphrased). Jesus's earthly ministry was all about bringing his Father's kingdom to this world. Every time he healed the sick, he brought heaven to earth. There are no sick people in heaven, so Jesus brought that reality wherever he went. There are also no demons in heaven. Notice how Jesus brought even this reality to the earth:

> But if it is by the Spirit of God that I drive out demons, then the kingdom of God has come upon you. (Matthew 12:28)

Jesus brought freedom from the enemy by bringing people into contact with God's kingdom. He revealed the Father's dominion and authority. Jesus's entire ministry was built on this principle, bringing the forgiveness, healing, and freedom of heaven to humans on earth. And this is the baton that he handed to his disciples when the Holy Spirit came with power in the second chapter of Acts.

Jesus, the Creative Son of God

When we look at Jesus's earthly ministry, we might struggle to spot creativity at work. Jesus said, "Very truly I tell you, the Son can do nothing by himself; he can do only what he sees his Father doing, because whatever the Father does the Son also does" (John 5:19). Some might think this meant he gave up on being creative and acted as a puppet. I think there's a better interpretation.

Jesus has always worked in tandem with his Father, even before he came to earth. When Jesus, the Word of God, brought the universe into existence, he was doing what he saw the Father doing. He was working in harmony with the Father, but he was still being creative.

I have a few friends with whom I like to record music. One, Bobby, plays guitar. All I need to do is sit down at the piano and lay out a basic chord structure, and he will add textures, layers, and solos that bring the song to life. Without my chord structure, he wouldn't have a pattern to follow. And even though I'm laying out the concept of what to play, he is partnering with me in the creative process, adding depth and nuance to the music that wouldn't be there without his collaboration.

In the same way, God the Father laid down the chord structure, if you will. Jesus joined in and operated within that concept and pattern, bringing life to the music in unique ways.

When Jesus told a parable, I don't believe he was repeating words from the Father like a mindless drone. Rather, I have the sense that he was taking the realities of heaven and creatively making them relevant and accessible to earthly people.

Notice that in Mark 4:30, Jesus started a parable by taking a moment to think about how to describe the kingdom of heaven. He asked, "What shall we say the kingdom of God is like, or what parable shall we use to describe it?" (See also Luke 13:18.) I picture Jesus staring into the sky while he searched for a creative metaphor. He knew what the Father was doing, and he knew how the Father works. Here, he simply needed to creatively convey that reality. The result was that truths from heaven were revealed in the earth. His kingdom came.

Jesus wasn't a puppet who somehow saw his Father superimposed on the world and merely mimicked everything he did. Rather, Jesus spent time in the Father's presence and thereby came to know his heart. From that place of relationship, he came to know what the Father was doing. In John 8:38, Jesus told a group of listeners, "I am telling you what I have seen in the Father's presence." In other words, he wasn't robotically repeating the Father. He had spent time with the Father and then found creative ways to express the heavenly realities he had encountered. Jesus was creative when he walked this earth.

I often wonder how much this principle applied to the ways he healed people. Did Jesus spit in the dirt and rub it on the blind man's eyes because he somehow saw the Father doing that? Or did Jesus perceive that the Father wanted to do something specific in this man's life, and then he creatively found a way to make that happen?

Personally, when I see a sick or injured person, I know that my Father wants to heal them. But rarely do I see a method. Instead, I go with the confidence of knowing what God wants to do, and I then say or do whatever seems right in order to accomplish that end.

This seems to be how Jesus did things. In John 5:21, he said, "For just as the Father raises the dead and gives them life, even so the Son gives life to whom he is pleased to give it." Jesus distributed life as he pleased—always in harmony with the Father, always subservient to the Father, and always revealing the Father, but still according to his own desire and will.

Creativity Produces Partnership

The first time I partnered with God to minister healing to someone, creativity brought the results. An intern at our church named Josh had developed an ear infection. Over the course of a few weeks without treatment (because, as an intern in 2009, he had no health insurance or money), it festered into a painful mess that had made him partly deaf in that ear. While I had seen God heal before, I had never yet been used to heal someone in Jesus's name with a command. Nevertheless, I preached about healing that night to the youth group and had the students pray for each other at the end.

A small group of seventh-grade boys prayed for Josh's ear, but nothing happened. He came up to me and asked, "Hey, they prayed and nothing happened. What should we do now?"

"Pray again," I answered.

We have a tendency to pray without results and then give up, reasoning that this must just be God's will. But I knew it wasn't God's will for this young man to be in pain or deaf in one ear. According to the prophet Isaiah, Jesus was wounded so that we can be healed. (See Isaiah 53:4–5.) Jesus cared so much about this young man's ear infection that he endured leather straps laced with bones and metal, tearing flesh from his own body. If he didn't want to heal, then he could have skipped that part of the crucifixion. But Jesus's sacrifice was complete.

So the boys prayed again and then came to ask me, "What should we do now? He's still not better."

"Pray again," I answered.

"But we've tried everything!" they replied in desperation—hoping to be let off the hook.

"Really? Everything? Tell me what you did."

"Well," they answered, "we prayed for him, we commanded the ear to be healed, and we told the infection to leave in Jesus's name—all while laying hands on him like you said."

With that, my creativity kicked into gear. I didn't have any sort of special revelation from God about how to help this young man experience God's healing power. I was merely trying to be funny and think of something the boys hadn't tried. To be honest, I wasn't even certain that it would work—I simply figured I couldn't look stupid since these guys had already "tried everything." I was merely trying to be a smart-aleck youth pastor and think of something ridiculous they hadn't tried. My creativity—in the form of humor—burst into action.

"You didn't try everything," I chided with a grin.

"What else is there?"

"Well, did you try this?" I jokingly strode forward to the intern sitting in his chair, poked my finger in his ear, and said, "Open!"

As I pulled my finger out of his ear, Josh's eyes widened. "Oh my gosh!" he exclaimed. "That worked!"

I think I was more freaked out than he was. "Are you serious? Don't toy with me!"

Sure enough, this young man was completely healed.

It wasn't because I saw the Father sticking his massive finger into Josh's ear. Rather, I knew that the Father was present to heal, and I was ready to persevere until this person experienced what God wanted to do. No one has an ear infection in heaven. By engaging in creativity, I accidentally received the joy and privilege of bringing a heavenly reality to earth. Creativity is one way that we can partner with our Creator.

In short, this story has become my license (excuse) for my ridiculous sense of humor. If God can work a miracle through me while I'm just trying to be funny (within his will, of course), then maybe I ought to make more such opportunities. One day, I believe my wife will finally agree.

The Spirit Gives Life to Creativity

God doesn't only empower our creativity; he also empowers his own. In the creation account, we don't see anything take shape until the Holy Spirit was present to empower it.

> In the beginning God created the heavens and the earth. Now the earth was formless and empty, darkness was over the surface of the deep, and the Spirit of God was hovering over the waters. (Genesis 1:1–2)

The Hebrew word used to describe the Holy Spirit hovering only appears three times in the Old Testament. The next time we see it, it is used to describe an eagle nurturing its young—stirring them up in the nest, protecting them, and then teaching them to fly. (See Deuteronomy 32:11.) The word could also be translated as "brood," "flutter," or "shake," which implies that some sort of movement and energy is involved. The word offers an image of bringing things to life.

I have heard a few different theologians and teachers suggest that the importance of the Holy Spirit hovering over the deep was that he may have been incubating the raw, subatomic materials needed for creation. Genesis 1:2 says that "the earth was formless and empty," which implies that the earth existed but had no real consistency or shape. If this is true, then it means either that the raw materials always existed (but were dead and without order), or that the raw materials were initially created by God but did not yet have any organization or life. I tend to think the latter is true since the Bible first says that God created the heavens and the earth and then specifies that the earth was formless. Either way, though, God saw fit to tell us that his Holy Spirit needed to hover over the surface of those materials before they could be given structure or meaning.

Only after we see the Holy Spirit hovering, brooding, and essentially vibrating over the surface of the deep do we find God declaring, "Let there be light." The implication is that even God the Father did not really create anything ordered or structured until his Holy Spirit was present to empower the work with supernatural life. Through the Holy Spirit's presence at creation, order was brought out of chaos, and the will of heaven was made manifest. The perfection, order, and life of heaven impacted the earth and brought radical transformation. Even God himself, in the moment of creation, was using creativity to bring heavenly realities to the earth.

If God didn't create anything apart from the Holy Spirit's movement and activity, why would we want to live any differently? Are we above God? The only way we will see spiritual life emerging from our creative activities is if we dive into the materials with authority from God and the supernatural life of the Holy Spirit.

> The Spirit gives life; the flesh counts for nothing. The words I have spoken to you—they are full of the Spirit and life. (John 6:63)

"The flesh counts for nothing." In the strength of your own flesh, mere human creativity will not amount to anything meaningful.

But "the Spirit gives life." When the Holy Spirit empowers you, your creative expressions have eternal value. God the Father knew this was vital, so he created the entire universe this way. Creativity, when empowered by the Holy Spirit, is life-giving.

God Hasn't Changed

God never stopped being creative. The same God who formed man from the dust of the ground also spit in the dirt to make mud that would form new eyes for a blind man. (See Genesis 2:7 and John 9:6–7.) The same God who opened Adam's side to create a wife also pierced Jesus's side and gave birth to his bride, the church. (See Genesis 2:21–22 and John 19:34.) God's projects may differ from time to time, but his creative nature doesn't change.

Furthermore, God never stopped giving creative gifts to mankind. The Israelites weren't the only ones to be empowered in this way. In the coming chapters, I will show you case after case of God's supernatural creativity bringing words, images, and more from heaven to earth through people like you and me.

During the Renaissance period in Europe, many of the artists and sculptors believed that their commission from God was to bring the beauty of heaven into this world. Some of the most breathtaking architecture on earth was developed by Christians who recognized the spiritual responsibility associated with their creativity.

Consider also how God has used the medium of music throughout history to bring glory to his name and transform hearts. Many times in ministry, someone can say something a hundred times from a church pulpit with no response, and then one of the people will come and say, "I was listening to this song, and God showed me something." Sure enough, it's the same topic the speaker had been hammering for months. On one hand, we can rejoice that the Spirit is moving. On the other hand, I wonder if maybe I should start singing my sermons and teachings. God certainly uses the arts.

Creativity Affects All of Life

Throughout history, God has used multiple art forms to speak to and through his people. Different people are moved in different ways, and it takes an army of Christians gifted with empowered creativity to present the gospel in ways that will reach everyone. You are a part of God's creative media army. You have skills, talents, and gifts that he can't wait to ignite with power from the Holy Spirit.

With that said, not all creativity is artistic in nature. Rather, you might use your creativity in the world of business. I'm not only talking about being a skilled craftsman, like a carpenter or welder. I'm also talking about people who dream up marketing strategies, ideas for new businesses, and ways to allocate funds more effectively. I'm talking about efficiency experts, research and development scientists, financial managers, and inventors. While we may not culturally see these as art forms, creativity is certainly essential to success in these fields.

Still others engage in creativity in relational ways. Good parents regularly discuss questions like, "How can we help our child get through this situation?" Husbands think of creative ways to love their wives. Wives think of creative ways to bless their children. Friends think of creative activities to do together. And in the church, we are always looking for creative ways to reach more people with the gospel of the kingdom.

Whatever forms of creativity you engage in, the focus should be on bringing heavenly realities to earth. How can you bring the peace, love, and harmony of heaven into your family? How can you bring the love-filled strategies of heaven into your business? How can you impact this world with what you already know to be true about your Father in heaven? How can you add texture and melody to the chord pattern produced by our Lord?

You have the mind of Christ (1 Corinthians 2:16). You are united with him in spirit (1 Corinthians 6:17). You don't need any new special revelation to partner with him. You simply need to be the new creation He made you through Jesus.

God empowered the Israelites to craft replicas of heavenly objects without ever seeing the originals. In the same way, he desires to empower you to creatively bring the realities of heaven to earth and reveal his heart to mankind. As you yield to him, you may not even realize that you're being used in this way. But if the children of Israel are any indication, God doesn't need you to have all manner of spiritual experiences in order to bring heaven to earth; you simply need to be empowered by him and take a step of faith.

He will empower your creativity. Let him.

CHAPTER 2

THE PROPHETIC POTENTIAL OF CREATIVITY

God is not bound to audible language; it may not even be his preferred way of speaking. The prophetic can be powerfully released through actions and movements as the mode of communication.

—Dan McCollam

One day, God told the prophet Jeremiah to take a little trip down to the house of a local potter, saying, "I'll give you a message there." Upon his arrival, Jeremiah watched as the potter's clay started to fall apart on the wheel. So the potter took that same clay and formed a new pot. That's when God spoke to Jeremiah about what he was about to do for the nation of Israel. (See Jeremiah 18.)

God used the process of creativity to speak prophetically to Jeremiah. The process—not the finished product—had prophetic significance. As you engage in the creative process—no matter your medium—often times, God will speak. This is largely because creativity itself is a prophetic act that reveals the nature of God. Whenever a person is being truly creative, people marvel. I believe the reason is that they are catching a glimpse of a part of God.

This doesn't only apply to our observations of other people. I often find that God speaks to me as I write. In fact, I received some of the more significant revelations he has given me while I was in the process of writing. I often hear God more clearly while engaged in the creative process than when I'm just reading, so I'll usually write down thoughts as I read the Bible (or another book) to keep myself engaged in thinking creatively and listening for his voice.

Engaging in healthy creativity brings us near the heart of God because creativity is part of his nature. Part of being Christlike is being creative. For the Christian who has union with our Father in heaven, creativity enables us to draw from that relationship and produce expressions of our Father's heart.

Prophetic Productions

The prophetic potential of creativity is not limited to its process but can also be realized in the product. Consider what God asked the prophet Ezekiel to do.

> Now, son of man, take a block of clay, put it in front
> of you and draw the city of Jerusalem on it. Then lay siege

to it: Erect siege works against it, build a ramp up to it, set up camps against it and put battering rams around it. Then take an iron pan, place it as an iron wall between you and the city and turn your face toward it. It will be under siege, and you shall besiege it. This will be a sign to the people of Israel. (Ezekiel 4:1–3)

Throughout my childhood, my dad built Lionel train sets—typically filling an entire room of our house. I would often join him in the train room to hold wood, run wires, and help position buildings and scenery. Ezekiel may not have known what a train was, but I imagine him building his model of Jerusalem with the same attention to detail as my dad gave to his trains.

God gave Ezekiel specific instructions about what to draw on the clay tablet; then he was instructed to build a model around the tablet to demonstrate what would happen to Israel. The result was a visual prophetic word that told the whole story at a glance.

In some ways, this may not seem very creative because God gave such specific instructions. But think about it: God didn't tell Ezekiel how many camps or battering rams; nor did God tell him what they should look like or where they should go. Ezekiel, with direction from the Holy Spirit, dove into a creative project and produced a visual prophecy.

Imagine what this means for you. The Lord might lead you to make a model of your house, neighborhood, city, or state; and then he might give you instructions for what to do with that model as a means of prophesying. You might write a song with prophetic lyrics. You might start a business that somehow prophesies the wisdom of heaven into your community. Your creativity can express the voice of God.

One day, I happened across some old photos of a handmade model of my childhood church, Canton Calvary AG. I recognized the building instantly. What I didn't recognize was a second, much larger structure on the back property.

I asked my mom about the photos, and she told me that my dad had made this model because of a vision he had. According to my dad, it wasn't a literal building but a spiritual church that would be much bigger than Canton Calvary but somehow related.

At the time, no one quite knew what to do with the prophecy, and it was largely shrugged off. Some even said my dad heard wrong.

In 2011, my wife and I started a house church in our living room, and over the next decade, it grew and multiplied. In 2019, we officially organized our network of house churches as Roots Church and began reaching out to our community more purposefully. By the summer of 2020, we had tripled in size (yes, even during the craziness that was the year 2020) and began looking for a building we could rent for large twice-monthly meetings where all our house churches could come together. As it turns out, the perfect location was Canton Calvary.

In many ways, we've become one church with them, even though we don't attend their Sunday morning meetings. We give generously to them. We built them a new playground for kids. We help them with various projects and sometimes fill in for the pastor or worship leader on Sunday mornings. And at least once per year, we combine together for a large church service.

We have about ten times as many people in our church as they do. We wouldn't fit in the building if we all showed up, but most of our people attend house churches, and only about half come to our large meetings.

My dad built a prophetic model that would take about forty years to see fulfillment. And decades later, that prophetic message still encourages us and bears fruit as we partner with my childhood church.

Prophetic Creativity

The prophet Jeremiah observed someone in the process of creativity, not knowing what the Lord wanted to speak. And in Ezekiel's case, the prophet heard the word of the Lord first and then carried out obedient creativity as a prophetic act. In each case, God used design and media to bring a prophetic word to his people.

Why should we think that God is any different today? Especially in a culture where originality is so valued, why wouldn't we expect God to speak prophetically through creativity?

In my first book, *The Word of Knowledge in Action*, I wrote about an older woman who approached me after church one Sunday and asked me to pray for her husband, who was struggling with alcoholism. The Holy Spirit gave insight into the issue and opened the door for the woman to receive an encouraging word of prophecy.

Days before we ever went to her house to pray for her family, the Holy Spirit showed me a specific shape—sort of like a letter L. As I drew the shape on a piece of paper, he started to prompt me to draw an *X* in several places, which I did. I assumed I was looking at the footprint of their house. Then I felt like the Lord was saying to draw circles surrounding the shape to represent the angels he was sending to change the situation. Not knowing how many to draw, I actually started with a ring of circles and then thought, *Why not fill up the rest of the paper?*. I did everything as instructed—with the creative license he gave me—and continued to pray for this woman and her husband.

The next Sunday at church, the woman came up to me while I was playing piano after the sermon. We didn't really know each other at the time, but she said, "I've been praying all week about what you said, and I just felt like I should ask you if God has revealed anything else about the situation."

"Actually," I answered, "God can talk to you just as easily as he can talk to me, but I do think I may have sensed something."

I flipped over some sheet music and drew the shape just like before. "Does this shape mean anything to you?"

The woman looked quizzically at it and didn't recognize it at all. I asked if it was the footprint of her house, but she said her house was a rectangle. I was about to dismiss it as my own imagination, but then she called her daughter over to the piano and asked her if the shape meant anything to her.

"Yeah," said the daughter, "that's Dad's room in the basement."

Then I started drawing the X's.

"What's here?" I asked with each X. First was his bed, then his television, then the refrigerator where he kept his liquor. Then I put three X's in a small cluster, just as I had in the first drawing, and asked, "What's here?"

"That," she answered, "is the chair where Dad drinks all the time."

To make a long story short, a team of us went over to this family's house to pray while the husband wasn't home. In a matter of only a couple months, the woman's husband decided to give up his years of drunkenness and leave the basement to sleep once again in the room with his wife. About eight or nine years later, I ran into this woman and her husband at a church I was visiting. God had completely turned his life around and healed their marriage.

My drawing may not have been anything spectacular to look at, but this visual couldn't be expressed with mere words. Again, in Jeremiah's case, the prophetic word came as he observed the process of creativity carried out by someone else (someone who, I might add, probably didn't have a clue that God was speaking through him). In Ezekiel's case, God gave him specific instructions about what to do and what it would mean prophetically. And in my case, I just had a hunch that the shape I kept seeing in my imagination might mean something, so I drew it, and God revealed more with time. But to this day, what amazes me most is how God gave me the liberty to draw as many circles (angels) as I wanted. I was invited into the creative process with the Lord, and his word came to pass.

Prophetic Music

Canton Calvary, the church I was raised in, is Pentecostal. The scene throughout my childhood was all too familiar: At a certain point in the worship and singing, the music would break, and someone would shout out something like, "My children, my children …" What followed was generally a declaration of love, encouragement, or admonition in the first-person as God spoke to the church through a yielded human being.

Based on 1 Corinthians 12–14, we respect these verbal exclamations as prophecies. Still today, I love to hear a prophetic shout of encouragement from God, so please don't think I'm downplaying it. Nevertheless, this method of presenting prophecy seems to have overshadowed many other creative expressions of prophecy that we see throughout Scripture.

One such expression is prophetic song. God designed both music and our bodies, knowing full well how it would affect us.

Music stirs our emotions and is one of the fastest ways to bypass a person's intellect to connect with their heart.[2]

Yet many have separated prophecy from music. Why? Perhaps for practical reasons. In a large church gathering, we might not be able to hear individuals in the crowd above our sound systems and praise bands. In the Bible, however, music and prophecy were often interwoven. While it may not be practical for the average Christian to prophesy this way in a big church service, it shouldn't stop musicians and singers from practicing it at all.

Throughout the Psalms, we find songs that convey prophetic words from God. Consider, for instance, Psalm 50. Here, a man named Asaph sang a prophetic word from God—first to his people and then to the wicked. God's proclamation was revealed in song. The music didn't stop and wait for a prophecy; instead, God joined in the music by singing through a willing and yielded human vessel.

Apparently, Asaph's gift for prophetic song was handed down to the next generation. King David placed Asaph's sons and the sons of two other Psalm writers in charge of prophetic music in his kingdom.

---

[2] In Psalm 108:1, David declared, "My heart is steadfast, O God; I will sing and make music with all my soul." When Mary was declared "blessed" by her cousin Elizabeth for bearing the Messiah in her womb, she sang out, "My soul glorifies the Lord, and my spirit rejoices in God my Savior" (Luke 1:46–47). Music and emotions are closely connected.

> David, together with the commanders of the army,
> set apart some of the sons of Asaph, Heman and Jeduthun
> for the ministry of prophesying, accompanied by harps,
> lyres and cymbals. (1 Chronicles 25:1)

Asaph was a songwriter. Heman was a musician. And Jeduthun was himself a prophetic singer.

> Jeduthun … prophesied, using the harp in thanking
> and praising the LORD. (1 Chronicles 25:3)

I find it interesting that it says Jeduthun "prophesied, using the harp." This could be taken a couple ways: Either he played the harp while he prophesied, or his harp-playing was actually prophecy in its own right. I suppose it's debatable, but I have seen God revealed through musicians without any words being spoken or sung.

To prophesy is to speak on another's behalf, but one can just as easily play music on behalf of another. If God invented music, it only makes sense that there are songs in his heart that he has written—both with lyrics and without. Remember that he rejoices over us with singing (Zephaniah 3:17). When we come close to his heart and express his music, we can rightly call that prophecy. Prophetic song can take many forms; what matters is that God is revealed.

I can't tell you how many times I've been impacted through prophetic song. Prophetic music and singing fuel spiritual warfare. They soothe life's hurts. They accelerate sanctification and transformation. They can be tools for the Holy Spirit to convict us of sin and awaken our consciences. They encourage, admonish, and uplift. They bring comfort. They spur us onward. They rally the church to action.

If King David recognized the need to officially appoint prophetic singers and musicians in his earthly kingdom, how much more important are they today in Christ's heavenly kingdom? Let the prophetic singers and musicians arise! Let prophetic songs burst forth from the church! Let the emotions of mankind be gripped with the Word of the Lord!

Engaging in Prophetic Creativity

Singing is not the only form of creativity through which we can prophesy. We also have an example in the book of Acts where a Christian acted out a prophecy. As Paul prepared to go to Jerusalem, a prophet named Agabus showed up and did something strange. Taking Paul's belt, Agabus tied up his own hands and declared that the owner of the belt would be bound in the same way upon reaching Jerusalem. (See Acts 21:10–11.) Here, the medium of acting became a vehicle for the prophetic word.

I've seen people dance prophetically, write prophetic poems, draw prophecies, and more. The results have always been powerful.

Whatever your talent or skill—be it model-making, singing, acting, or otherwise—God can use it prophetically. Listen for the voice of the Lord and look for creative ways to express and reveal what he wants to do and say.

As you pray and seek the Lord throughout your day, don't shrug off images, words, or melodies that might pop into your mind. Instead, ask the Lord if they might mean anything. If you feel a confirmation in your heart that it does mean something, ask him what you're supposed to do in response.

Maybe he's just guiding your prayer. Maybe he'll want you to write it down for later. Maybe he'll give you a specific interpretation right away. Or perhaps he'll have you exercise your creativity with prophetic purpose.

You might build a model like Ezekiel or my dad, draw a picture like me, write a song, carve a sculpture, play an instrument, write a letter, develop a website, make a movie, perform a dance, or even start a business. Your only constraint is the love and nature of Jesus. What matters is simply that your heart is set on Christ and your purpose is to draw the attention of others to him.

CHAPTER 3

THE CRAFTSMANSHIP
OF GOD

For we are the product of His hand, heaven's poetry etched on lives, created in the Anointed, Jesus, to accomplish the good works God arranged long ago.
—Ephesians 2:10 (VOICE)

O ur God is a Master Craftsman. Step out into nature and look around you. God's majesty, glory, goodness, and all manner of other attributes are revealed in what he has made. (See Romans 1:20.) Whether it's the strength and fortitude of the mountains, the power of the sea, the life-sustaining sun and rain, or the beauty of a flower, he is made known through it all. We are surrounded by a breathtaking masterpiece.

With all the beauty and splendor of the creation around us, it's easy to forget God's favorite project. Consider David's words:

> When I consider your heavens,
>> the work of your fingers,
>
> the moon and the stars,
>> which you have set in place,
>
> what is mankind that you are mindful of them,
>> human beings that you care for them?
>
> You have made them a little lower than the angels
>> and crowned them with glory and honor.
>
> You made them rulers over the works of your hands;
>> you put everything under their feet. (Psalm 8:3–6)

The crown jewel of God's creation is mankind. Nothing else enjoys the privilege of bearing God's image and having a relationship with him. No other being—not even an angel—has been invited to participate in the Creator's authority over all other creation.

God's supernatural grace and mercy are divine tools through which Jesus Christ continues to mold and shape us. We are works-in-progress as we are each conformed into the likeness of Christ (Romans 8:29). Your salvation is not in any way based on *your* work but rather on *his* work.

> For it is by grace you have been saved, through faith—and this is not from yourselves, it is the gift of

God—not by works, so that no one can boast. For we are God's handiwork, created in Christ Jesus to do good works, which God prepared in advance for us to do. (Ephesians 2:8–10)

So many Christians strive endlessly to please God with our works, not realizing that he is already pleased with his own work: *us*. At Jesus's baptism, God the Father audibly affirmed, "You are my Son, whom I love; with you I am well pleased," and he said this before Jesus ever entered ministry (Luke 3:22). Jesus had not yet worked one miracle, preached one sermon, gone to the cross, or risen from the dead. He hadn't technically done anything that he was sent here to do, and yet the Father was already "well pleased" with him.

Is it possible to displease God? Absolutely. But speaking as a father myself, it is possible to be displeased with my children's actions while maintaining an overall approval of them as my sons. I discipline them not to make them into someone else but to help them become who I know they truly are.

God's pleasure in us is based first on his work, not our work. Assuming you're a Christian, he is pleased with you right now, not because of what you have done but because of what he has done and is continuing to do in and through you. Even if your recent actions have been displeasing to him, he still longs to draw you deeper into his heart because he is wildly, madly in love with you.

Just as Jesus was God's physical Son, you, too, have been granted sonship through Christ. He is well pleased with you.

Long before Jesus came, King Solomon had a grasp of this concept. After building the temple that his father, David, had envisioned, Solomon addressed the people:

> While the whole assembly of Israel was standing there, the king turned around and blessed them. Then he said:
>
> "Praise be to the Lord, the God of Israel, who with his own hand has fulfilled what he promised with his own mouth to my father David. For he said, 'Since the day I brought my people Israel out of Egypt, *I have not chosen a city* in any tribe of Israel to have a temple built so that my Name might be there, *but I have chosen David* to rule my people Israel.'
>
> "My father David had it in his heart to build a temple for the Name of the Lord, the God of Israel." (1 Kings 8:14–17, emphasis added)

To paraphrase this passage, God was basically saying, "I never planned for this temple to be built here, but I did plan David. With a heart of love for me, David dreamed of building this temple, and I will bless it because I dreamed him."[3]

---

[3] Bill Johnson, *Dreaming with God* (Shippensburg, Pennsylvania: Destiny Image Publishers, Inc., 2006), chapter 1.

This has tremendous ramifications for the ways we practice our creativity. It means that we don't have to agonize over whether we have special instructions from God. On the contrary, all we need is a love and passion for God like David had. Then, if it is in our heart to do, God approves because we are in his heart. "For we are God's handiwork, *created in Christ Jesus* to do good works" (Ephesians 2:10, emphasis added).

Purifying the Heart

With all that said, I need to offer a word of caution. Notice that I said we need a love and passion for God. Without that, the things we purpose in our hearts are not beneficial. Jeremiah 17:9 says that "the heart is deceitful above all things." We are only safe vessels for heaven's creativity so long as we are in Christ.

Notice what creativity can do in the hands of someone who does not love God:

> As for an idol, a metalworker casts it,
>> and a goldsmith overlays it with gold
>> and fashions silver chains for it.
> A person too poor to present such an offering
>> selects wood that will not rot;
>> they look for a skilled worker
>>> to set up an idol that will not topple. (Isaiah 40:19–20)

Just because creativity comes from God doesn't mean it can't be perverted or misused. Only those who live in union with Jesus have the capacity to consistently produce meaningful, beneficial creations.

> A good man brings good things out of the good stored up in his heart, and an evil man brings evil things out of the evil stored up in his heart. For the mouth speaks what the heart is full of. (Luke 6:45)

In the world, creativity is an expression of oneself. The pattern of the world is to want to be noticed, to make a name for oneself, and to want people to be changed or impacted by something one made. The pattern of the kingdom, however, is to lay down one's own life for the sake of Christ and choose to express him.

> I have been crucified with Christ and I no longer live, but Christ lives in me. The life I now live in the body, I live by faith in the Son of God, who loved me and gave himself for me. (Galatians 2:20)

For a Christian, creativity functions contrary to the way the world uses it. Expressions of self can only benefit the general populace when self is transformed through the resurrection power of the Holy Spirit to reveal Christ.

For the Christian, creativity reveals our Creator. Righteous creativity can only happen when we first see that our sinful self was destroyed at the cross and then embrace new life from the Holy Spirit.

> You were taught, with regard to your former way of life, to put off your old self, which is being corrupted by its deceitful desires; to be made new in the attitude of your minds; and to put on the new self, created to be like God in true righteousness and holiness. (Ephesians 4:22–24)

Healthy Expressions of the Flesh

The new self is "created to be like God in true righteousness and holiness," but our lives don't always measure up. Even though our old self is crucified and dead, our flesh remains, along with its own passions and desires. Our new self is in process, being conformed into the image of its Creator. (See Colossians 3:10.)

As Christians mature, we can generally identify the difference between when we're living according to our flesh and when we're living according to the Spirit. It's as simple as identifying the difference between death and life, chaos and peace.

> Those who live according to the flesh have their minds set on what the flesh desires; but those who live in accordance with the Spirit have their minds set on what the Spirit desires. The mind governed by the flesh is death,

but the mind governed by the Spirit is life and peace. The mind governed by the flesh is hostile to God; it does not submit to God's law, nor can it do so. Those who are in the realm of the flesh cannot please God. (Romans 8:5–8)

As you read the Psalms, you find an occasional place where David or another psalmist, under inspiration of the Holy Spirit, expressed their own broken earthly, human feelings—seeking violence and destruction for their enemies.[4] From what we know of Jesus, who perfectly revealed the Father and called us to love our enemies, this is an expression of the flesh (even though inspired by the Holy Spirit) more than of God's heart.

This was perfectly all right, though, because it was in the context of prayer and passionate pursuit of God. The psalmist's creative expression of his flesh was a means of fostering intimacy with God. And it was so pleasing to the Lord that he saw fit to include it in his Scriptures as these songs were handed down through the centuries.

You are welcome to express your flesh, but express your flesh to God because that's the proper setting for it. When you express your flesh to people, sin reigns. The focus is on you. But when you express your flesh to God, you position yourself to hear his reply and be transformed.

It doesn't matter if other people see you expressing yourself to God. In fact, it can inspire and strengthen their relationships

---

[4] See, for example, Psalm 55:1–15; 58:6–8; and 137:7–9.

with him. The Psalms often echo the cry of my own heart and thus draw me into prayer.

When you want to express your flesh, do so in the form of prayer—even if your method is nonverbal. A painting can become a prayer. A dance can be intercession. Instrumental music can be an outlet for all manner of emotions. Whatever media you want to use, direct your expressions of flesh toward God rather than to people. That way, they will still be productive.

As we commune with God in this way, he speaks the realities of heaven back to us—realities that he wants you to reveal in the earth. You can then go and express the measure of Christ that he has invested in you—you can express your new self, which is a new creation that looks like Jesus. Rather than expressing your old self to the world, you will be able to express Christ.

When we express our flesh to the world, our old self becomes magnified. When we express our flesh to God, our old self remains crucified.

Putting the Old Identity to Death

Creative people sometimes have a hard time surrendering. Many creative people carry an inner satisfaction about what we do and how we do it. This can make us perfectly content with the ways we currently live. We can be quite secure in our earthly identities, and so we have a hard time letting go of the kingdoms we've built for ourselves.

Most people prefer a God who accepts us just the way we are. While this is true in the sense that one can come to him without changing first, we must realize that once we've come to him, transformation is part of the package.

Creative people sometimes develop a false persona into which we pour all our time, emotions, and resources. We dress a certain way, speak a certain way, and engage in certain activities so that when people look at us, they instantly recognize which creative field we like to engage in. For example, you can usually tell the difference between a computer programmer and a heavy-metal musician. You can also tell the difference between a person who uses his creativity to write business plans and someone who is a movie star.

We like the idea of being associated with our art forms. We like the personal branding. There isn't technically anything wrong with that, but if people can tell you're a poet but don't know you're a Christian, you might want to figure out why your artistic persona is more obvious than your faith.

It is possible to look like Jesus while dressing like the world. I'm sure Jesus looked a lot like a carpenter. My point is that your identity is not found in your art form or line of work. Your identity is found in Christ. Creative people often invest so much of ourselves in developing an external persona that it becomes difficult to see ourselves as anything different. Imagine what would happen if Christians would invest as much of our time, talent, money, and heart into developing an external expression of Jesus.

Any perception of oneself that falls short of identifying with Jesus is not in line with your God-breathed destiny and purpose. Yes, you are an individual, but only in the sense that you are a unique part of Christ's body, the church—dreamed up by God for a unique purpose. You're a new creation—different from everyone else—but you are still an expression of the one divine man, Jesus Christ.

Every part of his body is essential and needed. Every part functions differently and has a distinct purpose. But every part of this body is still a piece of one Person. (See 1 Corinthians 12:14-27.) If you're not revealing Christ, then you're not really being part of his body; you're still living in pride. The flesh that we were born into is incapable of revealing a pure expression of Jesus apart from divine intervention. It must be brought into a place of surrender to Jesus.

Each of us must choose the kingdom of God over self. We must daily surrender the values of our own self-made kingdoms to embrace God's kingdom. The kingdom of God will cost you everything that you have and everything that you are. But what you gain from it is worth so much more.[5]

---

[5] In Matthew 13:44-46, Jesus shared two stories to illustrate this point. First was a man who found a hidden treasure in a field and then sold everything he had to buy the field. There's no way he could afford the treasure, but by purchasing the field, he gained the treasure too. The second story is about a merchant who sold everything he had to purchase a pearl. As a merchant, he would have been expecting a return on his investment, which means that it was worth more than he paid even though he paid everything he had. In both cases, the person had to sell everything to attain

Anyone who fails to see the value in God's kingdom will continue to put his or her trust in an inferior kingdom that will one day be exposed for what it is. Right now, God is lovingly reaching out to sinners, but a time will come when everyone who still values self over him will be destroyed. Consider what our loving yet heartbroken God said to the prophet Isaiah when Israel continued to reject him:

> All day long I have held out my hands
>> to an obstinate people,
>> who walk in ways not good,
>>> pursuing their own imaginations ....
> I will destine you for the sword,
>> and all of you will fall in the slaughter;
>> for I called but you did not answer,
>> I spoke but you did not listen.
> You did evil in my sight
>> and chose what displeases me. (Isaiah 65:2, 12)

A Dedicated Imagination

In the passage you just read from Isaiah, God said that these people pursued their own imaginations. Our own imaginations are good and God-given. Trouble only comes when we separate our

---

what they wanted, but they ultimately received a treasure worth so much more than what they put into it. The kingdom of heaven is the same way. It will cost us everything we are and have, but it is worth so much more than we will ever invest.

thoughts from God and exercise our imaginations on our own. Anytime we separate from partnership with God, the natural outcome is sinful activity. Anything that does not come from a trust-based relationship with the Lord is sin. (See Romans 14:23.)

The old you has a sinful imagination. The new you has the mind of Christ and therefore an imagination dedicated to him. (See 1 Corinthians 2:16.) The old you is dead and therefore only capable of producing death. The new you is alive and united with God and therefore capable of producing life. Nothing truly creative can come out of death. Only life can reproduce life. You must consistently choose to consider your old life dead and live as a new creation. (See Romans 6:11.) See yourself as the new creation that you are.

The new creation loves and honors God above all else. The new imagination is God-seeking rather than self-seeking. Our challenge is to remain in that mindset. When the human imagination is self-seeking, we are deceived into thinking that God approves of our lifestyles when he actually doesn't.

> The word of the Lord came to me: "Son of man, prophesy against the prophets of Israel who are now prophesying. Say to those who prophesy out of their own imagination: 'Hear the word of the Lord! This is what the Sovereign Lord says: Woe to the foolish prophets who follow their own spirit and have seen nothing!'" (Ezekiel 13:1–3)

The prophets of Israel were producing false words out of their own imaginations rather than partnering with God. Our Lord spoke against them and even called them foolish.

If we don't understand what it is to be a new creation, we may use this as an excuse to avoid using our imaginations altogether. But that's not what God wants. He has made you a new creation and given you the mind of Christ so that your imagination can be dedicated to him. The result is a capacity to dream and imagine in productive ways that beautifully promote our King and express and establish his kingdom in the earth.

The sinful self-life is bound to pride and already stands condemned as it opposes God. As Christians, that sinful nature is dead. If we keep indulging ourselves and refuse to embrace the real, abundant life God has placed within us, then we willfully refuse his grace and mercy. "Pride goes before destruction, a haughty spirit before a fall" (Proverbs 16:18). All the self-life must remain humbly surrendered to the cross. We do this by considering it dead (Romans 6:11).

All this sounds like we're giving up so much. In a sense, we are. In the same way Jesus called the rich man to give up the possessions he was idolizing, he calls creative people to give up the false identities that we have come to cherish and hide behind. We cannot continue pursuing our own imaginations, trying to impact people with weak creativity that is limited to our own earthly, self-centered identities. We must allow ourselves to be transformed into the likeness of Christ so that his power and love are freely expressed through us.

New Creations in Christ

Again, the cost is great, but what you gain from it is so much more. Jesus didn't merely die; he also rose from the dead. So if you have put your old life to death with him, then "the Spirit of him who raised Jesus from the dead is living in you" (Romans 8:11). If we've died with him, then we also receive his resurrection life.

> For if we have been united with him in a death like his, we will certainly also be united with him in a resurrection like his. For we know that our old self was crucified with him so that the body ruled by sin might be done away with, that we should no longer be slaves to sin—because anyone who has died has been set free from sin.
>
> Now if we died with Christ, we believe that we will also live with him. For we know that since Christ was raised from the dead, he cannot die again; death no longer has mastery over him. The death he died, he died to sin once for all; but the life he lives, he lives to God.
>
> In the same way, count yourselves dead to sin but alive to God in Christ Jesus. Therefore do not let sin reign in your mortal body so that you obey its evil desires. Do not offer any part of yourself to sin as an instrument of wickedness, but rather offer yourselves to God as those

who have been brought from death to life; and offer every part of yourself to him as an instrument of righteousness. (Romans 6:5–13)

When I was seventeen-years-old, this passage of Scripture changed my life. I had been addicted, depressed, and filled with rage. My life and emotions were in a tailspin, even though I knew how to wear a great mask for everyone else. I desperately wanted freedom from my sinful habits but couldn't find it, no matter how hard I tried.

Then I read Romans 6 and realized I didn't have to fight my sin with my own willpower. I could simply consider all those things dead and trust the Holy Spirit to raise me to new life in Christ. Then Jesus would live through me and reveal himself in my words, actions, and attitudes.

Jesus, the ultimate Creator, expressed himself as he designed another new creation. He transformed my life and made me into a person who looks like him. I'm not yet perfect. I'm still clay on the Potter's wheel. But every day I yield to him is a day that everyone around me can experience him in greater measure.

When a person realizes and agrees that his or her old life died with Christ, the Holy Spirit comes in and makes that person a new creation. This new creation is a representative of Christ. As part of Christ's body, each believer has a measure of Jesus to reveal that no one else has the privilege to express. The false identity of sin is replaced by the true identity of Christ. His Spirit is joined with our human spirit to produce someone who has never been seen before—a truly new creation. (See 1 Corinthians 6:17.) Thus, we represent him even in our individuality.

Once we are new creations in Christ, we are finally in a right position to express ourselves—as long as we realize that our new self is a revelation of Jesus (as processed through our own unique experiences, talents, and testimonies). We are still unique. We are still individuals. But now, we are alive in Christ. He is in us, and we are in him. A new union has been formed, and a new expression of Jesus is being released in the world.

Partnering with Jesus

I used to pray, "Lord, I want none of me and all of you!" My intentions were right. I technically wanted none of my flesh and all of Christ's nature. But the way I understood this prayer was that I wanted to be a sort of puppet for God—never thinking or imagining on my own.

I didn't realize that once I became a new creation, I was liberated to imagine and create in even greater ways than ever before. My creativity could now naturally express Christ within me.

I soon realized the fallacy of my prayer. God already had "all of himself" and "none of me," and he wasn't satisfied with that—that's why he created me! If God wanted "all of him" and "none of me," then he would have never created me in the first place. (And that applies to you as well!)

Instead, God wants all of him *and* all of us. New creations are not Jesus-robots who mindlessly follow instructions. Rather, new creations are those who have put off the sinful nature, clothed themselves with the nature of Christ, and now use all their unique abilities, faculties, and creativity as expressions of that new nature.

If you are a new creation, filled with the Holy Spirit, you are empowered to reveal Jesus in everything you do, including your expressions of creativity. Like the Israelite craftsmen who built the tabernacle and its furnishings, you can bring heavenly realities to earth. And like David, who loved God with undying passion, you can please God with whatever you dream up in your transformed heart.

So is your creativity revealing the old you? Or is it revealing the transformed new you, which glorifies Jesus? If it's your flesh at work, then you're falling short of God's purpose and power—unless, as I mentioned, those expressions of flesh are directed to the Lord in prayer. But if, through the Holy Spirit, your imagination is made new, then you are in prime condition to reveal Christ with your creativity.

CHAPTER 4

CREATIVITY AND WORLD TRANSFORMATION

We do not become culturally relevant when we become like the culture, but rather when we model what the culture hungers to become.

—Bill Johnson

When James and I released our first movie in April 2014, we had no idea that a year later, it would be featured on international television and shared all around the world. Besides that, we had no idea that the accompanying book we wrote with our other friend, Jonathan Ammon, would be read and put into practice by thousands of people.[6]

---

[6] Our movie, *Paid in Full*, can be ordered at SupernaturalTruth.com or streamed online at vimeo.com/ondemand/paidinfull. The *Paid in Full 40-Day Activation Manual* is available through Amazon or the website above.

The success of our movie and book paved the way for my tiny blog to become a full-fledged production company focused on developing Christ-centered media. Through writing, video, music, filmmaking, graphic design, web programming, public speaking, animation, and more, we quickly trained well over ten thousand people to minister healing within only two years.

We're aware of missionaries and secret Christians in China and several countries in the Middle East who have seen our film and passed it around to others, using the movie to train their underground churches to minister healing in Jesus's name. Another man used what he learned to minister healing to people via social media, leading many to the Lord in nations like Pakistan and Iran via Facebook. Still others have told us that the culture of their church has never been the same since they all watched our movie together and healings broke out after the film.

If there was ever any doubt in my mind that media can have a global impact, the past several years have settled the matter. The key is identifying what medium will have the most meaningful impact on the people you're trying to reach.

Once upon a time, Christians had a lot of success handing out gospel tracts—small pamphlets that explained the message of salvation. Then something happened in our westernized culture in which society reached a point of ad saturation. With so much free literature and junk mail arriving every day, gospel tracts have largely fallen out of favor. Today, the success of these handouts has waned, but I'm convinced that's only because God has new ways to impact our rapidly changing culture.

God still uses various forms of media in supernatural ways to transform the world, and he can certainly do it through you. Our success with filmmaking should be an indicator to you that we still live in a media-hungry culture. Your job is to creatively partner with God in producing something people want to see. Perhaps it's a movie like I made or an online video series. Perhaps it will be a painting that moves hearts or a song that shifts a culture. Even seemingly small acts or gifts, like baking cookies for a neighbor, can have a ripple effect throughout the world. Your creative act of love might lead to your neighbor's salvation and the subsequent birth of new ministries through them.

Culture is constantly changing. Perhaps by the time you read this book, two-dimensional video will be outdated. The church needs to keep pace with the culture. In fact, I would argue that we ought to be the culture-setters.

The Culture-Setting Church

I belong to a church that is unlike any church in our region. I know every church likes to say that, but in our case, it's actually true. We only gather for a big meeting twice per month. Our weekly meetings happen in homes.

Each house church is a church in its own right—baptizing new believers, sharing communion, serving and loving one another, making disciples, teaching, praying, worshipping, and so forth. But we are also united as one large network, providing training, equipping, events, resources, and camaraderie to each other on a large scale. Hundreds of people call our church home, even though we primarily gather in small groups of five to twenty people.

I first dipped my toes in the waters of house-church ministry in 2005. At that time, megachurches thrived—tens of thousands of people gathering weekly for a high-octane, tightly choreographed worship experience. Our little group had no smoke machines, no lights, no crowds, and no schedule. We didn't even have music until one of my friends started bringing his guitar. We were just a small group of friends meeting in my girlfriend's parents' basement.

But we made disciples faster than any form of church I had ever seen. Within a couple of years, we grew to multiple groups and about forty people.

In 2008, I delegated that church to one of the original participants and joined the staff at a large church that I had attended years before. I begged to start a house church of young adults, but the timing was never quite right. They needed my expertise in other areas first—sharpening the nursery ministry, strengthening the Wednesday night programs, and so on.

I felt like a rat in a cage. It was a great church with wonderful people, exceptional leadership, and high-quality programs. But I struggled as I created bulletin inserts and planned big events. After two years, I hadn't baptized a single new disciple, and I longed for the earlier days when new believers emerged from our bathtub on a regular basis.

In 2011, I began traveling ministry and finally started another house church. I was still part of that big church, but I was now free to follow what I knew the Lord was leading me to do.

Over the next eight years, that little group grew and multiplied until about forty of us officially organized as Roots Church in August 2019.

Our region, Metro Detroit, is saturated with large churches. There are five megachurches within a half hour drive and hundreds of smaller congregations along the way. But our region is less than 20 percent churched. We want to connect with the people who might never set foot inside a church building. And we believe that to reach the people no one else is reaching, we need to do the things no one else is doing.

This takes tremendous creativity. We can't use the same programs and curricula that other churches are running with great success. We've reinvented the wheel multiple times over. But the result is new believers and the return of many disenfranchised, unchurched Christians coming back into fellowship with the body of Christ. Miracles happen regularly. Whole families are being restored. Ordinary believers pray for people, heal the sick in Jesus's name, and share the gospel, making disciples and inviting them into their spiritual family. Every believer is encouraged to creatively partner with the Lord to honor him and accomplish his mission.

Other churches struggled to understand what we were doing. So much of our model was too far outside the box for some to comprehend. But then came the spring of 2020, as fear, propaganda, and legitimate concerns spread alongside a global pandemic. Churches all over the world closed their doors. I soon began receiving phone calls from pastors of large churches who wanted to understand what we were doing. Seemingly overnight, we went from fringe to cutting-edge. Our creative expression of church created a culture that, today in 2022, has spread to over fifty house churches in other countries throughout the world.

Many Western churches play catch-up with the world culture. We do what we've always known until we see a cultural phenomenon in the world, and then we copy it to attract people to our message. We see it in contemporary Christian music as a worldly musician or band produces an exciting new sound and then Christian artists replicate it with sanctified lyrics. As popular concerts implement light shows and smoke machines, churches bring those special effects into our sanctuaries and learn to use them too. These displays aren't bad, but this is indicative of a mindset in which we expect creativity and innovation to flow from the world to the church and not the other way around. But we are the head and not the tail (Deuteronomy 28:13).

Trendy Church

Is it right or wrong to have a trendy church? Let's assume that by "trendy," we are referring to the popular American ideal with fancy lights, big auditoriums, professional musicians, dynamic video integration, full-color bulletins, high-quality marketing, and so forth. Some would say that such demonstrations are unnecessary or even wrong. But let's reframe the question. Is God worthy of all those special efforts being used for his glory?

Absolutely.

The problem isn't with trendiness or technology. The problem is when those things replace the purpose of our gathering. If you suddenly had to yank away all that extra stuff (for example, if there were, a global pandemic that made people stay home), what would happen to the people of your church? As it is preached, is the gospel message strong enough to sustain them? Would there still be enough of the presence of God, healthy fellowship, and Spirit-filled teaching to keep the people coming? If so, then I say: Go for it! But if not, then the media itself isn't actually the problem.

Swing the pendulum to the other extreme, and we find some churches avoiding new media for the sake of not conforming. They take pride in being unlike the world. I ask this group, "If you suddenly started using media like these other churches, would it make your organization more effective at reaching the lost and discipling believers?" Unless you're part of a secret, underground church in a hostile or restricted nation, the answer is probably yes.

Media and marketing have a significant psychological and social impact in today's culture. When used in the right ways, the exercise of our faith is fortified, and the gospel is spread more effectively. When used in the wrong ways, we become distracted from our Lord and fall victim to worldliness.

As culture changes, so do the media that we employ to minister to that culture. For instance, in the days of Moses, we see craftsmanship, tailoring, jewel-setting, embroidery, sculpting, instrumentation, singing, and so forth. The impressive clothing of the priests, the colorful décor, the symbolism of the wood and metal objects, the regal trumpets, and the reverent rituals all welcomed the people into a mindset of worship and awe. And God blessed that use of media by personally showing up there.

By the time King David and King Solomon rolled around, the portable tabernacle didn't seem adequate to impress the culture with the majesty of God. It would have felt wrong for Solomon to build a grand palace for himself and leave God outside in a tent, even though that was God's design. So Solomon set to work building the temple that his father, David, dreamed up—complete with choirs and prophetic singers. He took the plans of the tabernacle and magnified them into a mind-blowing display of riches and majesty. There, too, the Lord showed up with glory. Different media—same empowered results.

When Jesus walked the earth, he took a completely different approach—primarily because he had a completely different mission. Rather than adorning a temple, he literally was the Temple. And contrary to what we would consider smart marketing, he occasionally told people not to tell anyone about the miracles he worked. He prayed in secret and often ministered in secret. But we can't deny that Jesus drew massive crowds numbering in the thousands.

At first glance, it looks like Jesus's medium of choice was storytelling, but he employed yet another bit of handiwork. From what I can gather in the Gospels, the crowds seemed to come to him for more than great teaching—actually, Jesus's parables were often so confusing that most people didn't seem to understand the message. (See Matthew 13:10–17.) More than teaching or storytelling, the word about Jesus seemed to spread on account of the miracles he worked.

I certainly don't want to diminish the value of his miracles, but one could say that these miracles were a form of media—a sort of workmanship that grabbed the attention of the masses and drew them into Jesus's teaching and preaching. Yes, miracles are an expression of the gospel—making them far more than mere media—but this does not change the fact that Jesus gained followers through thought-provoking, culture-shifting, power-packed works. In fact, he went so far as to say, "Do not believe me unless I do the works of my Father" (John 10:37).

Several hundred years later, as church buildings were sprouting up all over the known world with significant financial backing, the use of media began to focus largely on architecture. Prophetic and scriptural symbolism were built into the very design of the building so that anyone entering the structure—especially the illiterate peasants—could see the gospel revealed in an awe-striking manner.

Today, in our westernized society, we have musicians, graphic designers, video technicians, and polished preachers. As culture has changed, our forms of expression have changed. But the need for empowered creativity among God's people has remained constant.

Are any of these media better than others? Well, I would certainly say that Jesus's miracles are an essential part of the gospel and are therefore powerfully relevant in every era. But when it comes to the other methods of expression, the creativity of God's people met the cultural needs of the day. Today's electric guitars and stage lights wouldn't have been effective a few thousand years ago any more than the single-note trumpets and fancy robes would be effective in most of present-day America.

I'm not suggesting that we change the church to conform to the culture. Rather, I'm talking about the church addressing this culture with the gospel in powerfully relevant ways. Nevertheless, more than relevance, we need power. We need creative Christians producing media that grips the attention of onlookers long enough for them to encounter God. And we need to lead the way in this, not merely playing catch-up with the world.

Today, we live in a fast-paced, globalized society in which culture is hard to specifically define. In America especially, culture seems to change faster than the calendar year. We no longer live in the modern world of the 1900s. Our culture has become post-modern. In fact, many have argued that we're now post-postmodern, and we're not even sure exactly what that means. For the sake of simplicity, though, we'll stick with the former term.

The Advantage of Postmodernism

Few cultural analysts these days agree on how to define postmodernism, but the basic gist includes many concepts relevant to the topic of creativity. Since I'm not writing an analysis of culture as much as I am encouraging creativity in the church, I'll not take space to describe the many intricacies of postmodernism. Rather, allow me to simply point out a small handful of postmodern concepts that open the door for empowered creativity to be more effective now than ever before. Postmodern people value the following:

❖ dialogue more than lecture

❖ relationships over isolation

❖ individualism and diversity

❖ creative and artistic expressions of one's own unique ideas

❖ respectful discussions about spirituality

Your creativity is viewed in this society as an expression of your individualism; and the people of this culture—who long to have meaningful relationships—are eager to dialogue with you about what you have made.

In light of this, the most meaningful artwork tends to have depth, symbolism, and individuality attached to it—all of which promote dialogue. It's not enough to paint a pretty picture. What does it mean? How were you feeling the day you painted it? What is the symbolic value of the picture? Does it have any sort of spiritual significance to you?

People are often curious about the life behind the media. They want to know what makes the artist tick. Media, then, can become a launch pad for dialogue; and since dialogue is so treasured by this generation, people will actually listen to what you have to say as you engage in conversation.

Through this process, ideas are challenged, and convictions are formed. So when the topic turns to Jesus Christ and the active presence of his Holy Spirit, you've now opened the door for personal transformation in the life of someone else. That's important because personal transformation is the gateway to world transformation.

If you want your artwork and design to impact this postmodern generation, then you need to remember three things:

1. Let your individuality in Christ shine through. Don't be generic. Make sure your work has meaning.
2. Don't be afraid to use symbolism that doesn't make sense at first glance. Depth of symbols makes people curious and encourages them to ask questions.
3. Remember that as a Christian, your identity is in Christ. Therefore, your individuality is intimately interwoven into your faith. The two are inseparable. Make sure the symbolism you're conveying reveals Christ in you—the new self—rather than your old self.

You have a license to be as creative as you want to be within the context of your new identity in Christ. Use whatever media you have at your disposal to express Jesus in whatever ways you can. This will open the door for dialogue, which can snowball into world transformation.

Revealing the One True World-Changer

Paul and Silas were accused of "turning the world upside down." (See Acts 17:6 NRSVUE.) In reality, any effect on the culture around them was not because of their own strength or effort. Rather, it was the result of Christ in them. Consider how Peter and John reacted after healing the man at the temple gate:

> While the man held on to Peter and John, all the people were astonished and came running to them in the place called Solomon's Colonnade. When Peter saw this, he said to them: "Fellow Israelites, why does this surprise you? Why do you stare at us as if by our own power or godliness we had made this man walk? .... By faith in the name of Jesus, this man whom you see and know was made strong. It is Jesus' name and the faith that comes through him that has completely healed him, as you can all see." (Acts 3:11–12, 16)

The world isn't turned upside-down by powerless people doing mediocre activities. The world is turned upside-down by the

One who spoke that world into existence. When John the Baptist saw Jesus approaching, he declared, "Look, the Lamb of God, who takes away the sin of the world!" (John 1:29). If that's not an earth-shaking reality, I don't know what is!

Any ability the disciples had to impact this world was directly related to the measure of Christ expressed through them. Therefore, if you want your creativity to transform this world, it must be intimately tied to the person of Jesus Christ. As an integral part of his body, you have a piece of Jesus to reveal in this world that no one else has the ability to express. Therefore, your creativity can reveal a measure of Jesus that no one has ever encountered before.

Don't get me wrong—I'm not talking about some sort of new revelation that makes God out to be something different than the Almighty Being who we meet in Scripture. God is the same God today as he was on the first page of Genesis. When I refer to new revelations of Jesus, I'm *not* talking about a new Jesus. On the contrary, I'm referring to unpacking and revealing that which has remained true about him from the beginning, expressing timeless truth in fresh, creative ways.

For example, God's love is fathomless. No individual person—other than Jesus himself—could perfectly reveal all of God's love in a way that absolutely anyone would understand. Jesus can, but we can't. However, since we are all parts of Christ, I can reveal one facet of God's limitless love, and you can reveal another. The more Christians we have in the body of Christ revealing God's love, the more complete the picture of God's love that the world can experience.

A million people could preach about the truth and reality of God's love, and we would only have scraped the surface. Suppose, then, that a million more people painted pictures that revealed his love, and then a million more wrote songs about it. Add to that a million people with movies they made that reveal God's love and a million more with other spiritual gifts to reveal this love. We would still probably only be scraping the surface, but I can guarantee that the world would have a much clearer picture of who God is than when they were merely hearing words.

As the church steps out in greater creativity, the world is going to encounter a clearer expression of Jesus. God will become more tangible to them. Even though God has always been near, this—in the world's perception—makes him seem more accessible.

Your Piece of Jesus

You may be wondering, *Okay, Art, that's all good; but how do I know what part of Jesus I'm responsible to reveal?*

Actually, you may never know for sure until after the fact; but I can definitely show you where to start. John's Revelation teaches us that Satan will ultimately be defeated by (1) the blood of Christ, (2) Christians sharing the testimony of Jesus, and (3) people choosing to love Jesus more than they love their own lives. (See Revelation 12:11.) No matter where you are in your Christian journey, the one thing you have that is undeniably unique to you is your personal testimony.

Spiritual gifts, such as those listed in Romans 12 and 1 Corinthians 12, will emerge and develop throughout your Christian life as the Holy Spirit determines that you need them (1 Corinthians 12:11). You may not currently know what parts of Jesus you are called to reveal, but you do have a testimony to share as soon as you come to him. Every Christian, therefore, has something to express, no matter how small. Start by sharing your testimony, and the gifts will follow. (See Mark 16:20.)

Spiritual gifts—prophecy, healing, miracles, hospitality, and more—each reveal a piece of Jesus. As we discover spiritual gifts, God often gives us liberty to express those gifts creatively. Thus, we find ourselves revealing a unique measure of Jesus that no one else could possibly express (at least within this present time and space). Do not feel obligated to express spiritual gifts only in ways you have seen done before. Paint your prophetic words. Sing your words of wisdom. Use sculptures and drawings to minister healing to the sick. The only constraint is love, desiring for people to truly understand what God is communicating. (See 1 Corinthians 14:6–12.)

Again, if you're new to all this, you may not yet be practicing spiritual gifts. In this case, start with your testimony. Express it creatively. As you do, you may discover various spiritual gifts emerging that you weren't even trying to express.

When I started writing songs, I didn't even know what the term "spiritual gift" meant. But when I would perform the songs I had written, people would testify about how they had been impacted. I didn't even realize it, but some of my songs were prophetic messages. Others ministered healing. Others expressed gifts of encouragement. Again, I didn't realize that I was practicing spiritual gifts until later in life. These gifts simply emerged as I was faithful to loving God with my creativity.

When you express your personal testimony through creativity, the world around you will take notice differently than if you were to merely speak it. Our postmodern culture wants to understand the symbolism and meaning behind your creativity, and you will have opportunities to dialogue about what you have produced. Not only will your creative expression reveal Jesus, but your corresponding dialogue will make him plain. He will be revealed in your art form and through spiritual gifts. People will naturally take notice when Jesus shows up in power, granting you new opportunities to share the good news of God's kingdom in Christ Jesus.

In today's culture, creativity is a doorway to sharing the gospel. Thus, with the help of the Holy Spirit, your painting, song, dance, business, or whatever has the potential to turn the world upside-down. Engage this postmodern generation, and watch as God transforms lives and ultimately transforms the world.

CHAPTER 5

NATURAL TALENTS AND SPIRITUAL GIFTS

World evangelization was not to be done through the use of gimmicks or gadgets, but through miraculous signs manifested through the gifts of the Spirit.

—Gordon Lindsay

Spiritual gifts are supernatural abilities given to Christians by the Holy Spirit so that we can all benefit from revealing Christ in powerful ways. Jesus told us how the Holy Spirit operates, and this is key to understanding how spiritual gifts function:

> But when he, the Spirit of truth, comes, he will guide you into all the truth. He will not speak on his own; he will speak only what he hears, and he will tell you what is yet

to come. *He will glorify me because it is from me that he will receive what he will make known to you.* All that belongs to the Father is mine. That is why I said the Spirit will receive from me what he will make known to you." (John 16:13–15, emphasis added)

In the New King James Version, Jesus said the Holy Spirit will "take of what is Mine." (See John 16:14.) Sometimes he takes from Christ's healing power and makes it known to us—that's a gift of healing. Sometimes he takes from Christ's knowledge and makes it known to us—that's a word of knowledge.[7] Other times, he takes from Christ's extreme generosity and makes it known to us—that's a gift of generosity. Whatever the case, a gift of the Holy Spirit takes place when the Holy Spirit makes some aspect of Jesus known through a believer for the common good of everyone present. (See 1 Corinthians 12:7.) Spiritual gifts are mentioned throughout the Bible, but what matters for this chapter is that we understand that they are supernatural abilities given to human beings that would be impossible apart from the active presence of the Holy Spirit.[8]

---

[7] For a better understanding of the spiritual gift called a word of knowledge, check out my first book: *The Word of Knowledge in Action*, (Shippensburg, Pennsylvania: Destiny Image Publishers, Inc., 2011).

[8] Plenty of books have already been written about spiritual gifts, so I haven't taken a great deal of time explaining them in this chapter. My favorite book to recommend (at least until I write one!) is *The Spirit-Filled Small Group* by Joel Comiskey published in 2013 by CCS Publishing.

For the most part, many Christians tend to practice spiritual gifts in traditional ways. We lay hands on people to heal them. We speak or write prophecies, words of knowledge, encouragement, and words of wisdom. These seemingly conventional methods of practicing spiritual gifts are wonderful and effective, but a limitation to conventional methods is not found in Scripture. For example, Paul didn't only speak in tongues; he also sang in tongues (1 Corinthians 14:14-15). As stated in chapter 2, Ezekiel didn't merely speak a prophecy; he built a model of it. And Agabus didn't merely speak a prophetic warning to Paul; he also acted it out.

In the coming chapters, I will share numerous other biblical examples, including a sculpture that healed poisoned people, music that subdued demons, and woodwork that spoke prophetic destiny. Creativity was coupled with supernatural ministry throughout the Bible, and it is still useful in the church today.

When you use your natural talents to express a spiritual gift, the synergy produces a unique expression of Christ that grabs the attention of the masses in ways that mere words might never accomplish. Natural talents are no substitute for spiritual gifts but can certainly enhance them.

Suppose a woman receives a word of prophecy but doesn't feel that mere spoken words could adequately express the depth of the message in her heart. That woman could perhaps sing the prophecy to better convey emotion. If, however, she has no natural singing talent, her voice may capture people's attention well enough, but they will probably be distracted by the awkward sounds emanating from the howling prophetess. Suppose, though, that the woman is naturally talented in painting. Imagine the impact that she could make if she masterfully painted a picture depicting the prophetic word she received. This would captivate people in a wonderful way and spiritually minister to them.

Wouldn't it be great for miracles to happen as you play an instrument? What if people were healed when they looked at a picture you painted? What if you performed a theatrical monologue on stage and hundreds of people came to Christ? Natural talents can only do so much in the hands of ordinary people, but the possibilities are endless when those same talents are expressed through transformed, redeemed people who are empowered by the Holy Spirit. Your natural talents can become vehicles for the spiritual gifts God has given you.

When Spiritual Gifts Look like Natural Talents

I learned to the play piano in a week. I learned guitar in a month, flute in two hours, and saxophone in six hours. I picked up the harmonica in a few days and the trombone over a weekend. I even learned to play my mother's dulcimer while she was out grocery shopping. That's not to boast, except to show you what is possible when God wants to do a remarkable work.

The strange thing is, I was never very musically talented. I used to sing off-key. And when I played trumpet in my middle school band, I barely passed the class. At the end of sixth grade, I buried my trumpet in the back of my closet and decided never to pick it up again.

I know what you're thinking. How did you go from a failing band student to learning piano in a week?

It all started at a series of tent revival meetings at the little church where I grew up. As the week of outdoor church services drew near, my mom somehow convinced me to unearth my trumpet and join the musicians on the praise team. My protests about nearly failing sixth grade band fell on deaf ears. The next thing I knew, I was sitting in on practice, struggling to write down a simple harmony for each song. I wasn't very good, so I only alternated between two notes on each song. And whenever I felt particularly daring, I would add a third note.

As you might expect, it wasn't anything spectacular. But all the little old ladies in our church did what little old ladies do—they marveled over how spectacular the ninth grader with the trumpet was. I still wonder why I went along with it, but they somehow convinced me to stick with the band and play each Sunday.

Within a few months, I had started playing four notes!

Here's where the story gets a little weird. For months, I would finish playing my trumpet, set it down on a chair on the stage, and then go sit with my parents for the sermon. One Sunday morning, though, I thought, *I sure wish I had a trumpet stand so I look a little more professional.*

I climbed back into the junk corner of our church's upstairs sound booth and began digging through the forgotten relics, hoping maybe someone had discarded a trumpet stand there. That's when I found it: a custom-made instrument stand with a place for a saxophone, a flute, a clarinet, and—to my delight—a trumpet.

The stand had belonged to an elderly man named Dave Harkness who had passed away about five years earlier, so I figured he didn't need it anymore. Dave played many different instruments, but all I cared about in that moment was that I now had something better than a chair on which to set my trumpet.

But as I carried the stand to my spot on the stage, I remembered the story of Elijah and Elisha. As God took the prophet Elijah into heaven in a whirlwind, a piece of his clothing (called a mantle) fell from the sky and landed at the feet of Elisha. Picking up that mantle, Elisha knew he had received what he had asked for: a double-portion of the Spirit that was upon Elijah. (See 2 Kings 2:1–14.)

I looked at that stand and said, "Lord, please make this like Elijah's mantle, and I want a double portion of what Dave had."

That day, I played by ear like never before in my life. I ventured beyond my four notes and started playing melodies, harmonies, and fills. It wasn't perfect, but it was definitely a far cry from what I could do only a couple of hours earlier!

Within six months, I was playing ten different instruments. I then went with a team to reroof a church in northern Michigan. Naturally, I brought along the guitar I had learned to play only a couple of weeks earlier and played it around our campfire at night.

The pastor of the church—who didn't know my story—asked if I played piano.

"Why do you ask?" I replied.

"Well," he answered, "we have plenty of guitar players; but if you played piano, then I was thinking of having you play on the worship team this Sunday."

It was only Monday, so I figured a week should be enough time to figure out how to play piano. The pastor laughed at my youthful enthusiasm and thought I was joking.

Every time I had a break from working on the roof, I would sneak into the little church's sanctuary, sit down at their upright piano, and try to figure it out. That Sunday, I played piano during the worship service. Again, it wasn't perfect, but it was good enough to do in front of people.

The next Sunday, back at my home church, I played "Our God Reigns" while the offering was being received. When I started the song with a fancy run, my dad—in the second row—burst into a roaring belly laugh. He didn't know I had learned piano the previous week, so he thought a tape was playing and I was faking it. When I finished, he stood up in the second row, turned around, and shouted, "I'm sorry, everyone. I didn't know he could do that!"

At the time of this writing, I've now led worship all over the United States. People are always asking me if I give piano lessons, but the truth is that I can't read music. The Lord supernaturally gave me what I can only call a gift of music. It's not a natural talent even if it does look like one.

Gospel singer and songwriter Andraé Crouch has a similar story. Crouch's father had just become a pastor at a small church. On the first Sunday, he asked his eleven-year-old son, "Andraé, if God gave you the gift of music to play and sing for him, would you do it for his glory all your life?"

The young Andraé simply answered, "Yeah, Daddy."

Just a few weeks later, as the congregation was singing, Andraé's father called him to the front. "If you're gonna play," he said, "play!"

Andraé sat down at the piano and started to play. Now decades later, Andraé Crouch is known for writing classic songs like "Bless His Holy Name," "My Tribute," and "The Blood Will Never Lose Its Power."[9]

Another great example would be the craftsmen of Israel who were introduced in chapter 1. One could assume that the lead craftsman, Bezalel, developed his skills over time; but given my story and that of Andraé Crouch, I wonder if he, too, was supernaturally surprised with a spontaneous gift from God. In Exodus 31:3, God said that he had filled Bezalel with the Spirit of God and with "all kinds of skills." The way it reads, Bezalel's craftsmanship seems more like a supernatural gift than a natural ability.

---

[9] DivineUsInc, "Testimony- Pastor Andrae Crouch," excerpt from the movie *First Love: A Historic Gathering of Jesus Music Pioneers*, YouTube video, 7:24, September 4, 2012, https://youtu.be/zmPp8K7BeJY.

As you can see, sometimes spiritual gifts can look like natural talents. On the other hand, sometimes natural talents can look like spiritual gifts. For this reason, we need to have a proper perspective on natural talent.

Putting Skill in Its Proper Place

The trouble with natural talents is that they can function with or without the anointing of God while still tending to receive equal attention. For instance, plenty of songs are theologically inaccurate yet are accepted by many Christians due to high-quality musical arrangement. Many have joked that "good theology will ruin some of your favorite worship songs."

Many Christians will accept anything as true, so long as it is spoken, sung, acted, or otherwise performed with passion and skill. It has always seemed strange to me that many churches won't invite a random speaker without credentials to preach to the people, but the same churches will sometimes bring in a songwriter with even less experience and credentials. Creativity and talent often grant people favor that they might not otherwise receive.

> Do you see a man who excels in his work? He will stand before kings; he will not stand before unknown men. (Proverbs 22:29 NKJV)

This is not merely a spiritual principle; the same is true even in the world. In my previous career as a web developer, I was often hired to design and program websites for companies about which I knew nothing. I once designed a website and an entire marketing package for a company that invented technology for microbiological testing. They loved my work, but I still couldn't tell you exactly what their products did. Nevertheless, because of my talent (and some positive word-of-mouth), I wound up working in the presence of PhDs, MDs, and scientists. I was completely under-qualified to present that topic, but talent and skill opened the door for unmerited favor.

Later, they asked me to design diagrams that they could use to present an invention to investors. My friend, the scientist, explained the process, drew some rough diagrams, and asked if I thought I could handle it.

I said, "Let me see what I can come up with for you."

I went home, prayed, and asked the Lord to show me what this device was supposed to look like. I drew representations of microchips, pumps, tubes, lights, microbes, and more. The client was baffled by the finished product and extremely happy with the results.

I still couldn't tell you what the product did though. All I know is that God gifted me with insight that allowed me to put into practice the graphic design skills I've been developing over the course of my entire life.

I know many people in the church who go to the opposite extreme of saying that skill is not necessary—only a heart for God. Their message sounds noble but disregards many biblical examples.

In 1 Chronicles 15:22, we learn about a man named Kenaniah who was placed in charge of singing—not because he was the head Levite (which he was) but because he was skillful at singing.

Likewise, some like to quote the many Psalms that say in the King James Version to make a joyful noise. "All the psalmist asks for," they say, "is a noise; so don't worry about how it sounds. Just make a noise!" That's all well and good, but we can't overlook Psalm 33:3, which says to "sing to him a new song; play skillfully, and shout for joy." Those who aren't musical can shout for joy. Let the musicians play skillfully!

At the same time, I hold to the belief that worshippers are more important than musicians. If you have talent but no heart for God, I don't really want you to attempt to lead me in songs of praise to the Lord. If, however, you have a heart for God but no talent, I'm willing to wince through it and worship with you. You can't lead someone into something spiritual that you have not entered yourself. Jesus told his disciples that they could freely give away what they had received. (See Matthew 10:8.) You can't give what you don't have.

It is dangerous to put skill ahead of worship. In this environment, it is easy to slip into pride and start expressing the flesh through creativity. Rather than producing worship of Jesus, we produce worship of idols. Keeping Jesus first, however, helps us stay in line with our new, transformed natures, which reveal him in everything. True worshippers can make Jesus known without any skill at all; but prideful, self-glorifying people cannot effectively and consistently reveal him even with all the skill in the world.

Don't Rely on Natural Talents

The beauty of spiritual gifts is that they do not require any natural talent. If I am spiritually gifted in prophecy, for instance, I don't necessarily need a talent for public speaking.

Some of the people in the Bible who we might consider heroes were lousy speakers. Consider Noah, who preached for a hundred years and only wound up with seven converts from his own family. (See Genesis 6–8.) He was a great shipbuilder who clearly heard from God, but it doesn't look like he was very persuasive in his public speaking. Or how about Moses who is said to have had a stuttering problem or other such speech impediment? (See Exodus 4:10.) Or what about the apostle Paul who preached such a long and apparently boring sermon that a young man fell asleep, tipped out the second-story window, and died on impact? (See Acts 20:9.)

Paul was very clear that natural talents weren't necessary for him to present the gospel.

> When I came to you, brothers, I did not come with eloquence or superior wisdom as I proclaimed to you the testimony about God. For I resolved to know nothing while I was with you except Jesus Christ and him crucified. I came to you in weakness and fear, and with much

trembling. My message and my preaching were not with wise and persuasive words, but with a demonstration of the Spirit's power, so that your faith might not rest on men's wisdom, but on God's power. (1 Corinthians 2:1–5)

Paul invested more of himself into demonstrating God's power than he did developing public speaking talents. When the young man fell out of the window and died, Paul ran downstairs, threw himself over the man, and witnessed the power of God raise him back to life. I think it's funny that Paul's sermon wasn't recorded. No one remembers what he said—it apparently wasn't noteworthy. What we do remember, though, is that the dead guy came back to life! Power is far more valuable than talent!

You may feel as if you have no talent at all, but this should not stop you from expressing spiritual gifts; and it certainly shouldn't stop you from being creative. Creativity is our family business. Our Father has the market cornered on true creativity, and we participate in its practice throughout the world.

Turn Your Talents into Tools

What is your talent? What are you good at? What natural skills do you already have? Whatever they are, why not couple them with your spiritual gifts?

By all means, if God tells you to speak a word of prophecy, don't waste time trying to paint it. Be obedient. But if you don't have particular instructions about how something should be expressed, think about whether one of your natural talents might be a better vehicle for expressing the gift. God gives you a certain measure of liberty in expressing him; so unless he gives you specific instructions about how to convey his message, feel free to think outside the box. You may find that the gift has greater influence when somehow expressed differently than mere words.

CHAPTER 6

THE KEY TO POWERFUL CREATIVITY

The obedience that comes out of listening to God puts us scarcely in our truest vocation.
It is a radical place to be … No longer slaves to sin, but alive to God's voice, we are
brought into that spacious place of genuine creativity.

—Leanne Payne

C reativity and craftsmanship go hand-in-hand with warfare. In Scripture, God used the ingenuity and skills of ordinary men and women to win many battles for his people, both conventionally and unconventionally.

In conventional warfare, Israel fought using weapons and armor. Where would all those swords, spears, shields, breastplates, and helmets come from if it weren't for the blacksmiths, leatherworkers, and other craftsmen who creatively and skillfully made those items? Today, we don't really think about these things in terms of creativity, but back then, it was an art form.

Then we have unconventional warfare, in which God used unexpected methods to win victories for his people. Sometimes it involved worshippers leading the way, shouting, smashing clay pots, sounding trumpets, or simply walking.

Consider, for instance, the battle of Jericho. The Israelites marched around that walled city for seven days in silence, following the ark of the covenant, which skilled craftsmen made. On the seventh day, when they had finished marching around the wall, they blew shofars—trumpets fashioned from ram horns. With the trumpet blast, the Israelites let out a loud shout. The wall crumbled, and they took the city.

Or how about Gideon? He and only three hundred men took the entire camp of the Midianites by simply blowing trumpets, smashing clay pots on the ground, raising their torches, and shouting. God brought such confusion on the enemy that they turned their swords on each other.

These stories couldn't have happened apart from the craftsmanship of everyday people. As we saw in the first chapter, it took empowered creative people to handcraft the ark of the covenant before the Israelites could follow it around Jericho. Then there were the shofars, which were made from rams' horns that each had to be cleaned and carved (never mind the creative person who originally came up with the idea to use a ram's horn to make noise in the first place). We also have the torches, which each had to be crafted by hand.

Consider also the clay pots that Gideon's army smashed. Did you ever think about the fact that someone had to physically sit down at a pottery wheel and shape every one of those pots? They also had to be baked correctly or else they wouldn't produce any sound as they made contact with the ground. I don't think the Midianites would have been very startled by a loud *squish*.

The forms and expressions of creativity vary from story to story, but there's one common element throughout. This one common ingredient is the key to powerful creativity. Whether in conventional or unconventional warfare, the Israelites' success was not based on their creativity itself but rather on their obedience to the voice of God. Through obedience, their creativity yielded powerful results. The key to powerful creativity is obedience.

The Weapons of Our Warfare

When it comes to natural warfare like that of the Israelites, there is no such thing as a weapon that was not somehow influenced by creativity. In an obvious sense, tools like swords, spears, and axes had to be fashioned by hand. In a less obvious sense, we find weapons that didn't have to be formed by anyone—as when Samson simply grabbed the jawbone of a donkey and used it to kill a thousand Philistines. (See Judges 15:15.) Even in these cases, though, you must admit that creativity played a role. I would say Samson was pretty creative to grab such an obscure piece of a skeleton and use it as a weapon. And I suppose you could say that God's creativity designed the donkey in the first place. The point is simply this: In natural warfare, all weapons meet the battlefield through creativity.

The same is largely true when it comes to spiritual warfare. In Christianity, we have a very different battlefront. Our warfare is against an invisible enemy who fights with different rules. Make all the swords, spears, guns, and grenades you want—none of them will be effective against this enemy. The battle must be fought with different weapons.

> For though we live in the world, we do not wage war as the world does. The weapons we fight with are not the weapons of the world. On the contrary, they have divine power to demolish strongholds. We demolish arguments and every pretension that sets itself up against the knowledge of God, and we take captive every thought to make it obedient to Christ. (2 Corinthians 10:3–5)

In the larger context of 2 Corinthians 10, we find that this statement about taking thoughts captive has nothing to do with my own efforts to take my thoughts captive (although that's still a great practice). When you read the surrounding verses, you learn that Paul intended to come to the Corinthians and, through preaching, take their thoughts captive. The weapons of our warfare have an ability to demolish arguments and pretensions that stand against the knowledge of God in the hearts and minds of other people.

When James and I made our first movie, we had no idea that this simple, creative project would take captive the erroneous beliefs of Christians around the world. Our little film became a mind-renewer that has changed the thinking of tens of thousands, making their thoughts about healing obedient to Christ. Our movie may exist in the physical realm, but it isn't a carnal weapon. It is mighty to the tearing down of mental strongholds where healing is concerned. That's not a commercial; it's an observation. So many believers around the world have told us how their entire understanding of healing ministry has changed since watching our film, reading our book, or processing through the small group curriculum we developed.

As much as God used our skills and creativity to develop our movie, I know the idea behind it was conceived in the mind of Christ long before it was in our imaginations. We didn't invent the idea of training and equipping believers.

The weapons we fight with don't have their origins in this world. This means that they cannot be invented by ordinary human minds. If our actions are to have divine power, then they must have divine origin. In spiritual warfare, all supernatural weapons are first conceived in the mind of God.

Consider the ark of the covenant. Not only was it part of bringing the walls down at Jericho, but the Old Testament is full of situations where God's power was demonstrated through the ark—

proving that it was more than just a fancy box. For example, remember that the Jordan River parted as the priests who carried the ark waded into the water. (See Joshua 3.)

One of my favorite stories about the ark took place when the Philistines captured it and brought it back to their city. They put it in their temple in front of a massive idol representing their god Dagon. The next morning, Dagon was flat on his face before the ark. They stood him back up, but the next morning he was right back on his face—and this time, his head and hands had broken off. The Philistines moved the ark from city to city, and everywhere it went, the people were plagued by an outbreak of tumors. Finally, the Philistines agreed to send the ark back to Israel. (See 1 Samuel 5.)

The ark of the covenant may have been built by creative people, but it was first conceived in the mind of God. Remember, Moses saw the pattern of things in heaven and gave the basic instructions to the craftsmen of Israel. While the ark was not a natural weapon, it was still a natural object made by human hands. Even so, it carried a supernatural, spiritual power with it.

Again, all spiritual weapons are conceived in the mind of God. Therefore, if we want to put these weapons to use, we need to tune into the mind of Christ and listen to the voice of our Father. Then, through our submission to the King, we can engage in the creative process and expect that heavenly realities that carry power to fulfill their purpose will take shape on earth.

A friend once shared a testimony about a time when the Holy Spirit specifically instructed her to bake some brownies for her neighbor whom she had never met. In obedience, she baked the brownies and went to the neighbor's house. The neighbor invited her in and, in no time at all, was sharing all the struggles she was having in her life. This friend of mine had an opportunity to pray with the woman and lead her to Christ.

Brownies didn't win the spiritual victory, but they were the spiritual weapon God used to break down the wall separating the two women. Any ordinary person could have shown up with brownies and been spiritually ineffective, but brownies in the hands of an obedient, Spirit-empowered believer brought profound victory.

It seems strange to think of brownies as a spiritual weapon, but look at the supernatural effect that they had. God didn't tell my friend how to make the brownies; he simply said to make them. The brownies (and their purpose) were conceived in the mind of God. The creative process was then carried out in the context of obedience, and the result was a spiritual weapon that demolished a social barrier and led to a woman's salvation. Again, the key to powerful creativity is obedience to God.

Obedience in Action

There are two basic types of obedience to God: obedience to his revealed Word and obedience to his present word. God's revealed Word is that which has already been spoken, specifically in the Bible. His present word, which is still consistent with the life and nature of Jesus, is not necessarily found in the Bible but is rather spoken with clarity today.

Obedience to God's revealed Word is important and necessary, but it isn't enough. Plenty of Bible-believing people in the world are attempting to obey God by following all the biblical commands of Christ; yet they are often still missing the point. True obedience to God is not possible as long as we attempt it in our own strength. As soon as we try to obey in our own effort, we have already become disobedient because of pride. God opposes the proud, so we ultimately wind up defeated.

This is why we need to obey his present word, which is vital to the Christian life. Sometimes God has instructions for us that his revealed Word doesn't offer. For example, there's nothing wrong with television, but for a season in my life God instructed me not to watch any television for about six months. I would have missed that transformational season if I weren't listening for God's present word.

In Scripture, God's revealed Word was that all fruit is good for food, but his present word to the Nazirite was to abstain from grapes and their byproducts. (See Genesis 2:16 and Numbers 6:3–4.) And while God's revealed Word generally sends believers into all the world, his present word kept Paul out of Asia and sent him specifically to Macedonia. (See Mark 16:15 and Acts 16:6–10.) The present word doesn't contradict the former but rather brings people into alignment with Christ's will for the moment.

108

The revealed Word of God is the default plumbline for how we should live, but the present word of God offers us daily guidance in specific situations. Sometimes God wants tighter constraints on our lives. Sometimes God wants us to take specific action in situations where the revealed Word only offers broad principles.

We should follow the principles of the revealed Word whenever we're not sure of God's voice. The present word, however, involves an awareness of his presence here and now. What is he doing? What is he saying? Where is he going?

All this brings us to a sobering realization: Even if you could successfully obey every guideline of God's revealed Word, you would still be judged as disobedient if you did not follow his present words. The Pharisees tried to follow God's revealed Word to the letter, but Jesus rebuked them for being unaware God's present actions. (See Luke 12:54–56.)

Even though the revealed Word is more important for matters of life and doctrine, God's present word will judge us in the end. Even those who obey the revealed Word—prophesying, working miracles, and casting out demons—can discover at judgment that they lacked relationship with Jesus. (See Matthew 7:21–23.) If the present word is so critical, you're missing the mark if you don't obey it. God's presence is more important than his principles.[10]

This is why Jesus's sacrifice is so vital to us. We are saved by grace, not by works. Jesus is our righteousness. As we give our lives to him, he gives his life to us. Suddenly, we are no longer judged on our success or our inadequacy. Instead, our Father in heaven sees the beauty of Christ's work in us and welcomes us into his family. Rather than needing to prove our obedience, God simply calls us obedient because Jesus was and is obedient.

This grace does not exempt us from the need for active obedience. On the contrary, it should encourage us that obedience is our new nature and is therefore natural and easy. As a Christian, it is against your nature to sin.[11] We can now engage in active obedience to God as an expression of love and worship.

Our obedience doesn't save us, but it is an indicator of our love for God. God saves us from sin, death, and eternal judgment—not because of anything we have done but simply because he loves us. In return, we obey God because we love him.

If you want to successfully obey the present word of God, you absolutely must understand some simple biblical principles from his revealed Word: (1) In your weakness, he is made strong,

---

[10] GOD TV, "Living in the Presence vs Living by Principles | Bill Johnson," YouTube video, 4:18, September 13, 2021, https://youtu.be/yWmAnLNBzWQ.

[11] Ephesians 2:3 tells us that "we *were* by nature deserving of wrath." It's a past-tense reality because our nature has been changed. Now, through God's promises, we "participate in the divine nature" (2 Peter 1:4).

(2) with God, all things are possible, and (3) true obedience is the byproduct of a genuine love-relationship with Jesus Christ.

1) In My Weakness, He Is Made Strong

First, we must see that real spiritual strength—and therefore the ability to participate in the spiritual battle happening around us—is only possible in the strength of Christ. This strength can only be ours when we admit our own weakness.

> But he said to me, "My grace is sufficient for you, for my power is made perfect in weakness." Therefore I will boast all the more gladly about my weaknesses, so that Christ's power may rest on me. That is why, for Christ's sake, I delight in weaknesses, in insults, in hardships, in persecutions, in difficulties. For when I am weak, then I am strong. (2 Corinthians 12:9–10)

Many of us have the mindset that we can obey on our own. We recognize what we are supposed to do, and then we run off to fulfill the command in our own strength. The problem with this mindset is that our own strength is never sufficient to fulfill the commands of God. Jesus said we couldn't do anything apart from him (John 15:5). That is why he gives us his Holy Spirit to empower us.

If you want to truly be obedient to God, the first thing you need to do is ask him for help. When God tells you to do something, the healthiest response is to say, "Okay, but I need you to empower me for the job"—then jump into action. Spiritual work requires spiritual power. The works of the flesh are always insufficient. If you want to obey God, you need to first recognize that his power is only available to those who will first acknowledge their own weakness.

To illustrate this, take a look at Paul's words about how he went about spreading the gospel: "To this end I labor, struggling with all his energy, which so powerfully works in me" (Colossians 1:29). Notice that it was Paul who "labored," but the "energy" was God's. We do the work, but God provides the energy, strength, and supernatural power to enable us.

True obedience is only possible when we are empowered by the Holy Spirit, and this takes place when we admit our weakness and rely on him.

2) With God, All Things Are Possible

At the ripe old age of five-hundred-something, a man named Noah was given an impossible task. God found the one righteous man left on the earth and saw fit to use whatever woodworking skills he had to engage in the creative process. The result was the first ocean-liner—and probably the first floating zoo.[12]

Not only was the boat itself an insurmountable task but there was nothing to prove that a worldwide flood would ever happen.

---

[12] The story of Noah can be found in Genesis 5–9.

By faith Noah, when warned about things not yet seen, in holy fear built an ark to save his family. (Hebrews 11:7)

As you listen to the voice of God, you may find yourself called to carry out a project, mission, or action that seems completely and utterly impossible. But harkening back to our previous principle—that we must acknowledge our weakness and ask for God's strength—there is nothing that God cannot do. If he calls you to do something, he will empower you to fulfill the mission.

Jesus looked at them and said, "With man this is impossible, but not with God; all things are possible with God." (Mark 10:27)

When I first started traveling ministry in 2011, the Lord prompted me to host a school of ministry over the summer. I thought the task was bigger than I could handle. But once I organized the training location and wrote the curriculum, the dream became a reality. From the very first week of teaching, the Holy Spirit was present, participating in everything I did. What seemed beyond my capabilities wound up being entirely possible with motivation and empowerment from the Holy Spirit. God used my talents, skills, and spiritual gifts to produce a discipleship program that trained people in full-gospel ministry.

Years later, in 2019, when we wanted to start a school of ministry for our church, I already had a base of knowledge and experience. My co-pastor JonMark Baker and I organized the Roots School of Ministry, which just finished its third year and has trained about one hundred people to know God, make disciples, plant churches, and minister in the power of the Holy Spirit. And next year, we intend to adjust the curriculum yet again to make it more accessible to the average Christian. Without empowered creativity, this task would be an impossible burden. The Holy Spirit loves to help birth God-given dreams.

3) True Obedience Comes from Loving Jesus

God is not a dictator, demanding obedience from his minions. Rather, he is a loving Father who desires for his children to receive the blessings of obedience. A wrong view of God can cause us to strive for approval rather than rest in his love. God's love for you is not based on your success or obedience. Rather, your success and obedience are based on your loving relationship with God.

> Jesus replied, "Anyone who loves me will obey my teaching. My Father will love them, and we will come to them and make our home with them. Anyone who does not love me will not obey my teaching. These words you hear are not my own; they belong to the Father who sent me." (John 14:23–24)

Some people look at this verse as though Jesus was manipulating his disciples, saying something like, "You had better prove your love to me by doing what I tell you to do. If you don't obey me, I don't believe you love me." But that's not at all consistent with what we know to be true of Jesus.

On the contrary, Jesus was saying, "If you will simply love me, you will find that obedience will be the natural byproduct. If you're having trouble obeying me, consider the root of the issue and work on your relationship with me. If you don't love me, you're going to have a hard time doing what I ask you to do. Love makes obedience possible because in the context of this love, I will give you the Holy Spirit."

> "If you love me, keep my commands. And I will ask the Father, and he will give you another advocate to help you and be with you forever—the Spirit of truth." (John 14:15–17)

If you truly love Jesus, all the resources of the Holy Spirit are available to empower you to obey his commands and teachings.

Obedience flows from love because love comes from knowing God and encountering his love for us. (See 1 John 4:19.) When we know God, we naturally love him. In that place of relationship, he calls us obedient. And since it is impossible for God to lie, obedience becomes our new nature. We are new creations who are designed to love and obey God as his Spirit empowers us to do the impossible.

Consistent Victory

Musician and songwriter Jason Upton hit the nail on the head when he wrote that victory only comes from a pure heart.[13] The secret to a consistently victorious life is a pure heart before the Lord that keeps us sensitive to his voice. If your heart isn't pure before the Lord, your creativity will often reveal your flesh rather than the will of God. But a pure heart, which is only possible in the context of a love-relationship with Jesus Christ, will reliably produce victory for the kingdom of God. Power walks hand-in-hand with purity.

God gave Israel the creativity needed to accomplish his will, even in the context of natural warfare. But creativity can also work against God's will. Consider the fallen creativity expressed in Nazi Germany. Some documentaries describe some of the secret weapons programs that the Nazis were carrying out. Without trying to give them too much credit, they truly were being creative with the weapons they were developing. But the heart of their mission wasn't pure, and the result was total defeat. Creativity coupled with an impure heart of disobedience is devious and leads to discipline (and if uncorrected, this will ultimately lead to judgment), but

---

[13] Joshua [Recorded by J. Upton]. (2002). On *Jacob's Dream* [CD]. Key of David Ministries.

creativity coupled with a pure heart of obedience brings supernatural victory.

God alone brings the victory—not our craftsmanship. Our creativity can either produce weapons of the flesh, which war against the Spirit, or weapons of the Spirit, which war against the flesh and the kingdom of darkness. The determining factor is our love for Jesus. If we love him, our creativity will flow from obedience. Through a pure heart that loves the Lord Jesus, your creativity can become the tool or vehicle through which God expresses his eternal triumph.

What is your craft? Graphic design? Music? Web development? Filmmaking? Painting? Business? Photography? Cooking? Public speaking? Illustration? What is it? Where is your talent? You may feel like it has nothing to do with spiritual warfare, but when coupled with obedience to the voice of the Lord, it will be powerful.

If you want your creativity and craftsmanship to be used by God in effective spiritual warfare to bring victories according to his will, then seek his face and listen to his voice so that you can respond in obedience. Take the time to develop a love relationship with Jesus Christ. He is more than ready to win supernatural victories through your empowered creativity.

CHAPTER 7

OVERCOMING THE ASSAULT AGAINST CREATIVE PEOPLE

There is a glory to your life that your enemy fears,
and he is hell-bent on destroying that glory before you act on it.
—John Eldredge

A s a creative person who bears God's image, the armies of darkness want to destroy you. I don't say this to scare you but rather to alert you to the spiritual battle taking place all around you.

The enemy knows that creativity is a powerful spiritual weapon in the hands of a Spirit-filled Christian. The enemy has no chance at victory—Jesus has already won the victory once and for all. However, Satan knows his time is short and that his best plan of attack is to strike down the people who cause him to lose the most ground. I'm not giving the devil credit; I'm just stating the facts.

This is why we see such an assault against creative people. It's why popular musicians are so often tempted by money, sex, and drugs. It's why artists are often sabotaged by the very institutions that train them, as nudity and sensuality seem to be unavoidable. And consider all the creativity that's possible through computers— graphic design, animation, digital recording, and so forth. Is it any wonder the internet is littered with so much pornography and sin? The devil wants to do all he can to destroy God's creative image- bearers.

Nevertheless, I am convinced that the church is invited to go on the offense rather than the defense. We cannot allow the battle to merely happen to us. We must dive in with clarity, vision, and purpose.

Stop Fighting with Gardening Tools

This assault against creative people is nothing new. The idea was practiced in the natural, physical realm thousands of years ago.

King Saul faced an ocean of Philistine warriors with his little army. The Israelites were sorely outnumbered, and the Philistines decided to kick them while they were down:

> Raiding parties went out from the Philistine camp in
> three detachments. ... Not a blacksmith could be found
> in the whole land of Israel, because the Philistines had

said, "Otherwise the Hebrews will make swords or spears!" So all Israel went down to the Philistines to have their plow points, mattocks, axes and sickles sharpened. The price was two-thirds of a shekel for sharpening plow points and mattocks, and a third of a shekel for sharpening forks and axes and for repointing goads.

So on the day of the battle not a soldier with Saul and Jonathan had a sword or spear in his hand; only Saul and his son Jonathan had them. (1 Samuel 13:17, 19–22)

I'm not sure if this means that the blacksmiths were killed or taken captive, but the fact remains that the Philistines removed these creative people from Israel's army. As a result, the weaponless Israelites had to pay the Philistines to sharpen their gardening tools in hopes that they could fight with those.

When I was younger, much of Christian media seemed to function the same way. For instance, the secular world seemed to have all the good music. Christians seemed forced to either go to the world and copy their style or else come up with something inferior and try to sharpen that. In a very real sense, it was as though we were going to the Philistines to sharpen gardening tools rather than forging our own powerful weapons.

Thankfully, creative Christians have come a long way since then. Today, we see genuinely creative and innovative Christian artists of all kinds. We have new sounds of music emanating from the church, new movies, new multimedia presentations, and more.

Christians at large are starting to engage the culture with Spirit-filled creativity, and it is changing the face of the planet.

Which group do you want to look like? Are you content to merely copy the world and pour all your resources into the world system only to wind up with inferior gardening tools? Or will you seek to know the creative Christ—in whom are hidden all the treasures of wisdom and knowledge—and be transformed into his image by the Holy Spirit? (See Colossians 2:3.)

The scriptural mandate to die with Christ has nothing to do with suppressing your God-given abilities. Rather, it has to do with embracing the full potential of those abilities by partnering with God. The church needs our creativity. The world needs our creativity. You carry within you a God-designed weapon that is devastating to the kingdom of darkness.

We must guard against the enemy's ploy to remove creativity from the body of Christ. If the devil can keep the creativity of Christ in heaven and out of the earth, he can essentially paralyze the body of Christ. He's not powerful enough to keep it there on his own. His only real tool is lies. We each have the free will to either agree or disagree with his assertions. The devil can try all he wants to paralyze the church, but if we stand on truth, then he has no power. Do not accept the lie that creativity is for the world. That would be like the Israelites joyfully handing over their blacksmiths and swords to the Philistine raiders.

Thankfully, many believers today are producing truly unique music, movies, books, graphics, and more. I love seeing the variety of expression with which God has filled his church. Christians are indeed rising up with superior spiritual weapons rather than trying to copy the world.

Nevertheless, many of us still haven't discovered our true potential in Christ. Many of our blacksmiths remain captives of the enemy. The church needs our creative people producing spiritual weapons. One classic revival song from the 90s encourages us to go to the "Enemy's Camp" and repossess all that has been stolen from us.[14] Our blacksmiths don't belong under the devil's thumb; the devil belongs under our feet.

Pay Attention to "Who" You Are Making

Paul said that Jesus Christ exists in and through all things and that "in him, all things hold together." (See Colossians 1:17.) We also know that his invisible attributes are revealed through what has been made. (See Romans 1:20.) Therefore, what God created when he made the universe was an expression of himself. The Lord put himself into his work. God set an example for us that all of his creation was about a "who" rather than a "what."

In the same way, everything you make—whether you realize it or not—is about a who. Either we are revealing Christ by serving God with renewed minds and Spirit-filled creativity, or we are creating idols that reveal the enemy or simply our own flesh. It's always about you, the enemy, or the Lord. It's always about a who.

---

[14] Black, R. (1997). Enemy's Camp. Integrity Inc.

Throughout Scripture, idols were all about serving self. Even if the spiritual focus of an idol were a demon, the purpose of forming that idol or serving that god was not to merely make the demon happy; it was to gain something in return—whether thriving crops, riches, a spouse, protection, or any number of other blessings.

In an effort to serve self, those who make idols reveal and express false gods. In contrast, those who purpose to serve Jesus Christ naturally engage their creativity in revealing and expressing the one true God.

Are you serving yourself or serving the true God? To answer this question, you must determine the purpose of why you are doing what you are doing with your creativity. If the purpose is all about you, then you're making idols to serve yourself. If the purpose is all about loving God and revealing his love to others, then you're making revelations of him. God is revealed in our creativity when we walk in a love-relationship with him.

In Christianity, our God is always pleased with his children, and he is always excited to welcome more into his family. Our God is in a good mood. He isn't unapproachable, and he certainly isn't waiting for us to mess up so he has reason to destroy us. If that were the case, Jesus would have never bothered to come into the world. There is nothing you could do (or not do) to make him love you more or less. He is infinitely loving, and he does not show favoritism. (See Acts 10:34; Romans 2:11; and Galatians 2:6.) The things we do for our God are not for personal gain or to manipulate him. We simply do them because we love him. They don't earn us any special favor, and they don't force his hand to bless us. They simply minister to his heart and bring him greater pleasure.

Many people, however, live according to law rather than grace. They live in fear of doing the wrong thing, thus angering their god(s) and bringing judgment upon themselves. In turn, they do what they can to please their god(s) in hopes that it will result in blessing.

Most of us probably don't create literal idols, but we do often use our creativity in idolatrous ways. Rather than using our talents and ingenuity to serve God, we use these things to serve ourselves. This selfish activity may have to do with money, fame, accolades, attention, success, or simply inner satisfaction. These things are not wrong in themselves—God often blesses people with all these things—but when any of these become the driving force behind our creativity, we have entered into idolatry. We have made false gods to serve us rather than loving the true God and resting in him.

So, who are you making? Are you making idols, or are you making expressions of Jesus? Does your craft, artwork, or other activity provide for the advancement of our Father's kingdom (financially, relationally, experientially, or otherwise)? Or does it merely serve you?

Engage in the Battle

Returning to our story, the Israelites were horribly outnumbered by the Philistines. Their mere six hundred soldiers with gardening tools were up against three thousand chariots, six thousand charioteers, and soldiers outnumbering the sands on the seashore. The two armies camped out on either side of a large canyon for days until a young man named Jonathan finally tired of the standoff.

Jonathan and his father, King Saul, were the only Israelites left who had swords. Saul hid in his tent, not wanting to stir up any trouble—basically awaiting the impending devastation from across the gorge. On the other hand, Jonathan grabbed his armor-bearer and crossed the canyon, and the two of them killed twenty Philistines in the area of about half an acre.

To use this as a metaphor, Saul represents the person with a sword of creativity who serves self—avoiding conflict and trying to survive in a place where the enemy is successfully stealing, killing, and destroying. In contrast, Jonathan represents the person with a sword of creativity who serves God—his or her mind is set on victory and freedom for others.

As Jonathan and his armor-bearer engaged in battle, God caused a great earthquake. The Philistines became confused and started killing each other. The Israelites saw the Philistine army "melting away in all directions." The tiny group began to look at the situation through a lens of hope and quickly joined the fight.

King Saul led the charge, and those who had been in hiding soon followed.

People like to do things that work, so they aren't likely to jump onboard with a creative revolution unless someone demonstrates to them what is possible as they partner with God. Yes, it's happening already, but perhaps it still needs to happen in your church or region. You could be a Jonathan for those people.

In your hands is a sword of creativity. If you will engage in the battle, God will back you up by bringing supernatural victory just like he did for Jonathan. Naturally, others will be inspired to join. Before you know it, a whole army of Christians will be fighting alongside you, securing the victory that God has already established for his church.

Be the Blacksmith

Since creativity can be used so mightily in spiritual warfare, the enemy wants to destroy the creative people in God's army. If there are no blacksmiths, who will make the weapons? If there are no creative people, who will create spiritually dynamic media that has the power to transform the world?

Many of us have a tendency to take gardening tools to the enemy's camp for sharpening. We make inferior copies of the world's creativity because the world seems to be better at what we want to do than we are. It's time for those of us who think this way to repent and join the army of creative warriors who are already in action.

God wants to empower Christians to be on the cutting-edge of creativity—in music, graphic design, filmmaking, web development, writing, business, and so forth. The Holy Spirit wants to inspire Christians to take their media to a level far beyond where the world has gone in their own strength. This is the difference between being a blacksmith and simply taking your inferior tools to be sharpened by the enemy. One is powerfully creative while the other is merely an attempt to keep up with the other side.

But make no mistake, if you're going to be a blacksmith in God's army, then you're going to be a target! The army of darkness will pull out all the stops in an effort to undermine your faith. An assault of temptations will come your way. You must maintain your intimate relationship with God through Jesus Christ.

So cling to Jesus Christ and get out there on the cutting edge. Don't wait for the world to lead the way. Blaze a trail. Create spiritual weapons in the form of music, graphic arts, pottery, video, photos, paintings, websites, books, articles, blogs, businesses, dances, inventions, architecture, and more. Ask the Holy Spirit for inspiration and take action.

CHAPTER 8

CREATIVITY AND SUPERNATURAL POWER

God is made known through His works.
When his works flow through his children their identity is revealed,
and there is an inescapable revelation of the nature of God in the land.
—Bill Johnson

An atmosphere of creativity invites spiritual power. The question is, which power will be at work? Either the Holy Spirit will empower the work, or the enemy may board it like pirates. One way or another, all creativity invites spiritual power of some kind. This doesn't mean that everything in existence has spiritual power attached to it. It simply means that the potential is there, and everything that is not dedicated to God's service is up for grabs.

You may have heard it said that the devil isn't creative. As Jesus said, "The thief only comes to steal, kill, and destroy"—not to create (John 10:10). So when it looks like the devil is doing something new, he isn't. All the enemy can do is pervert and twist what God has given.

You can imagine, then, why the enemy puts forth such effort to influence the thoughts and perspectives of creative people. God has given human beings creativity, and the creative works of a person under the influence of the enemy will be contrary to the kingdom of God. As Paul said in Romans 1:30, "they invent ways of doing evil."

The enemy longs to infuse human creativity with spiritual powers of darkness. Consider, for instance, horror movies, which are nothing more than vehicles invented by fallen humans for distributing a spirit of fear. Likewise, pornography carries with it a spirit of lust. Advertising often proliferates the spirit of "mammon" (or materialism). War propaganda sometimes opens people's minds to spirits of racism, hatred, and murder.

You may recall in chapter 6 when I talked about creativity as a weapon. There, I shared the following Scripture:

> For though we live in the world, we do not wage war as the world does. The weapons we fight with are not the weapons of the world. On the contrary, they have divine power to demolish strongholds. We demolish arguments and every pretension that sets itself up against the

knowledge of God, and we take captive every thought to make it obedient to Christ. (2 Corinthians 10:3–5)

Strongholds are arguments, ideas, mindsets, and mental structures built of thoughts. And these structures allow the enemy access to our lives. In Ephesians 4:26–27, Paul warns us, "Do not let the sun go down while you are still angry, and do not give the devil a foothold." Anger is one of those structures in the mind that creates an access point for the enemy.

Is it any wonder, then, why so many people who spend their time watching cable news and similar programming end up living in such deep deception? They watch hours of people arguing while the anchors basically tell them what they need to be angry about. They entertain themselves with outrage, and the devil plants his hooks. All the creative work of graphic designers, writers, camera operators, sound engineers, set designers, lighting specialists, and TV personalities converge to create a stronghold-generator that influences the masses.

Creative people create and destroy strongholds. The devil doesn't have to be creative in order to magnify the kingdom of darkness. All he needs are people with creativity who are living in rebellion against the God who gave it to them.

On the other hand, we have Christians, filled with the Holy Spirit and demonstrating the power of God in this earth. We too have creativity. And just as the enemy longs to attach his minions to misguided human creativity, so our Father in heaven is happy to bless the creative efforts of his obedient children, demolishing strongholds and planting seeds of the gospel.

Spiritual Power and Physical Objects

The desert sun blazed overhead. The people would have been sweating bullets if they weren't so parched. Without regard for lessons they had already learned, they began to question the quality of their leader and the faithfulness of God.

"We want bread!" they demanded. "And how about some water? We ate better when we were slaves! What kind of so-called freedom is this?"

These Israelites following Moses should have known better. These were the same people who saw the earth open up and swallow the families of Korah, Dathan, and Abiram for griping about Moses. Just after that, 250 people were consumed by fire, and then 14,700 people died of a plague until Aaron interceded for them. (See Numbers 16.) But they clearly hadn't learned their lesson, and God—in faithfulness to his righteous law—brought discipline by sending venomous snakes into the Israelite camp. (See Psalm 119:75.) The people repented, and Moses prayed for them.

Strangely enough, God didn't simply make the snakes go away. Instead, he commissioned Moses to make a metal sculpture—a bronze snake—that could be hoisted up a pole. Anyone who was bitten by a snake and then looked at the bronze sculpture would be healed. (See Numbers 21:4–9.)

God didn't tell Moses what to make the snake look like. He simply said to make a snake. Moses entered the creative process, and the finished product brought healing to anyone who looked at it.

It is entirely possible, then, that as you pray for someone to be healed, God may respond by having you engage in creativity and craftsmanship. God wants to empower some of us today to creatively handcraft sculptures and other crafts that bring miraculous healing to all who see them. Like Moses's snake, these crafts will be prophetic pictures of Jesus.[15]

Unfortunately, with power-packed craftsmanship comes the danger of idolatry. A time came when the venomous snakes were no longer an issue, but Moses's sculpture was still hanging around. The people named it Nehushtan and began to worship it and burn incense to it. That is, until King Hezekiah finally destroyed it. (See 2 Kings 18:4.)

The name given to the snake sculpture means "a thing of brass," but the root word carries with it a concept of lust and harlotry.[16] The bronze snake had changed from an item devoted to the purposes of God to an item that led people away from God. What was originally designed for good was stolen by the enemy and used for evil. Since the people weren't in any condition to

---

[15] Jesus said that the bronze snake on the pole was a symbol of himself. See John 3:14.
[16] *Brown-Driver-Briggs' Hebrew Definitions*, (Peabody, Massachusetts: Hendrickson Publishers Marketing, LLC., 1999)

simply change their minds on the matter, the only solution was to destroy the snake.

We learn from this story that the heart behind creating something only goes so far. Even though something was created with good intentions by a godly leader, people can still willingly hand it over to the enemy.

In the same way, though, this means that some things currently devoted to the enemy can be redeemed for the kingdom of God. As with all aspects of creation, either a thing gets redeemed, or it gets destroyed. Some things can't be redeemed— like pornography. They simply need to be destroyed. But other things can be redeemed.

Various musical instruments—like electric guitars and drums—have been considered evil at one time or another because of their connections with evil. But in the hands of creative believers, these inventions can be redeemed for a noble purpose and used to advance the kingdom of God.

Even the cross itself—invented by the twisted minds of violent men—has now been redeemed. What used to be the most gruesome form of torture and execution imaginable is now a symbol of our freedom and transformation.

It is time to redeem creativity. It is time to reclaim the arts. It is time for the church to fully engage in the creative process. Perhaps you will be the one to make the sculpture that heals the sick. Perhaps you will be the one to invite the supernatural power of God through your sanctified imagination.

It wouldn't be a far stretch. Years ago, Bill Johnson told a testimony about a young person in his church who drew a picture of a shoulder and then drew a red circle with a slash, crossing out the shoulder. When they found a person with a hurt shoulder, they said, "Here hold this. Now how does it feel?" Incredibly, the shoulder was completely healed—and this happens time and time again with similar pictures![17] Can you imagine the doors this opens to talk about Jesus?

My co-pastor, JonMark Baker, recently told me a story from a street-evangelist he knows. An artist in his church sketched a detailed portrait of a woman's face, and then she went looking for her. As expected, she found the woman in the store, gave her the portrait, explained the gospel, and led her to Jesus.

Twice now, I have received reports from people who were healed while reading an article on my website, SupernaturalTruth.com. One of the men had a severe internal problem that was causing serious pain in his side. The doctors had run all the tests for simple things and were now about to run the tests for serious conditions. As this man read my article, he placed his hand on his side and received healing from the Lord. All the pain instantly left, and the doctors could find nothing wrong with him.

---

[17] Solid Rock Media, "Bill Johnson - Easter Sermon - I Tried (POWERFUL TEACHING)," YouTube video, 38:10, March 26, 2018, https://www.youtube.com/watch?v=4H3UMGaQdJo. This testimony is a general example of what people in his church (Bethel Church in Redding, California) are doing on an ongoing basis. Stories like this—with drawings bringing healing in Jesus's name—happen regularly.

Creativity that Proclaims Prophetic Destiny

Just as the people who looked at Moses's sculpture were physically healed, a design that speaks prophetic destiny will enable those who look at it to enter into that destiny.

In reality, this was the premise of the bronze snake. Remember, the snake represented Jesus on the cross (John 3:14). It prophetically spoke of victory over the serpent in the garden, salvation from the sting of death, and physical healing—all of which would be procured at the cross by Christ. This prophetic design brought the onlookers into an encounter with a future reality.

In the book of Genesis, we find an obscure story that isn't preached on very often. There's no beautiful moral lesson or doctrinal teaching. However, we know that God included it in his Word for a purpose. Here's the story:

> Jacob replied, "You know how hard I've worked for you, and how your flocks and herds have grown under my care. You had little indeed before I came, but your wealth has increased enormously. The Lord has blessed you through everything I've done. But now, what about me? When can I start providing for my own family?"
>
> "What wages do you want?" Laban asked again.
>
> Jacob replied, "Don't give me anything. Just do this one thing, and I'll continue to tend and watch over your flocks. Let me inspect your flocks today and remove all

the sheep and goats that are speckled or spotted, along with all the black sheep. Give these to me as my wages. In the future, when you check on the animals you have given me as my wages, you'll see that I have been honest. If you find in my flock any goats without speckles or spots, or any sheep that are not black, you will know that I have stolen them from you."

"All right," Laban replied. "It will be as you say." But that very day Laban went out and removed the male goats that were streaked and spotted, all the female goats that were speckled and spotted or had white patches, and all the black sheep. He placed them in the care of his own sons, who took them a three-days' journey from where Jacob was. Meanwhile, Jacob stayed and cared for the rest of Laban's flock. (Genesis 30:29–36 NLT)

So Jacob was cheated by his father-in-law; but earlier, he had received the family blessing (or birthright) from his father, Isaac, which meant that God wanted him to prosper. What action would Jacob take to fulfill God's blessing on his life? Frankly, he did something that many of us would call superstitious. I call it creative. Either way, it worked!

Then Jacob took some fresh branches from poplar, almond, and plane trees and peeled off strips of bark, making white streaks on them. Then he placed these peeled branches in the watering troughs where the flocks came to drink, for that was where they mated. And when they mated in front of the white-streaked branches, they gave birth to young that were streaked, speckled, and spotted. Jacob separated those lambs from Laban's flock. And at mating time he turned the flock to face Laban's animals that were streaked or black. This is how he built his own flock instead of increasing Laban's.

Whenever the stronger females were ready to mate, Jacob would place the peeled branches in the watering troughs in front of them. Then they would mate in front of the branches. But he didn't do this with the weaker ones, so the weaker lambs belonged to Laban, and the stronger ones were Jacob's. As a result, Jacob became very wealthy, with large flocks of sheep and goats, male and female servants, and many camels and donkeys. (Genesis 30:37–43 NLT)

Jacob whittled away at some wood and used his handiwork to speak prophetic destiny over certain sheep. He claimed all the strong offspring for himself and prospered as a result. The sheep were constantly kept aware of their destiny through the logs Jacob designed, and God used that tool to produce physical results.

There wasn't anything special about the whittled branches, the bronze snake, the article on my website, or the evangelistic drawings on their own. The objects themselves didn't have supernatural power. But as artistic representations of the Lord's prophetic word, they kept the promise and purpose of God before the sheep and the people in a tangible form. God used those items as instruments and was pleased to use creations that his children had made with their own hands.

Creative Equipping

Ephesians 4:11 tells us about five ministries that Jesus has distributed into the church: apostles, prophets, evangelists, pastors, and teachers.[18] Verses 12 and 13 tell us that these people are given to the church for a specific purpose: "to equip his people for works of service, so that the body of Christ may be built up until we all reach unity in the faith and in the knowledge of the Son of God and become mature, attaining to the whole measure of the fullness of Christ."

In summary, that means Jesus has given these people to equip others to express the fullness of Jesus.

Apostles, then, are given to (among other things) train and equip other Christians to carry out the apostolic ministry of Jesus,

---

[18] Some theologians point out that this is arguably four ministries, not five, as some translations combine the last two roles into the title of "pastor-teacher." I personally favor the idea of these as separate ministries because I have observed people who were effective pastors but not necessarily skilled teachers, and others who were great at teaching but not necessarily at leading people. Furthermore, the term "teacher" is used independently in Acts 13:1 in a way that seems to imply there are not teachers in every single church. Nevertheless, we understand that every church probably has shepherds of some kind. (And if not, the people are usually actively looking for such a person.) Admittedly, an individual could indeed fill both roles, just as Paul was both an apostle and a teacher (2 Timothy 1:11). But this does not mean that all apostles are teachers or that all teachers are apostles. For these reasons, I will be referring to five equipping ministries rather than four.

which includes preaching the gospel wherever they go, making disciples, representing God as his ambassadors, and ministering the gospel with signs and wonders accompanying.

Similarly, prophets are given to equip other believers to hear the voice of the Lord and grow in intimacy with him—first by speaking the words others may not be hearing, second by confirming what others are hearing, and third by teaching others (through word and example) how to draw near to the heart of God and tune our ears to his voice.

In the same way, evangelists also have a role in equipping believers. Evangelism is the commission of every believer, so we know that the role of the evangelist is not merely to evangelize the lost. Rather, it is to articulate the Good News of Jesus and his kingdom to the church—training, equipping, and encouraging Christians with practical tools and ideas that will make them more successful in spreading the Word.

The Greek word for "pastor" is literally translated as "shepherd." These people are specifically gifted with an ability to lead, protect, and care for others while simultaneously having a remarkable ability to train and equip believers to lead, protect, and care for each other.

And teachers do more than teach information but also equip Christians to effectively and meaningfully teach each other (as Paul said the Roman church was capable of doing in Romans 15:14).

What we don't often talk about, however, is how these ministers can do what they do through creativity and media. The only creative expressions of these equipping ministries seem to be found in the form of writing and public speaking. But I'm believing for something more.

In the autumn of 2012, my friend and ministry partner James Loruss came to me with an idea. He was in his senior year of college and studying film music scoring, and he needed to select a final project that pertained to his major.

James said, "I want to make a documentary about physical healing and then score the music for it. Then my whole class has to watch a bunch of miracles in order for me to receive a grade!"

I loved the idea. To make a long story short, James and I began brainstorming ideas.

It wasn't long, though, before my passion for equipping people crept into the picture. I know I'm called by God to equip others for ministry, so it wasn't enough for me to film a bunch of testimonies and miracles. I wanted to train the viewer how to do the same things and greater.

We immediately began shaping the film around the idea of training and equipping everyday Christians to minister healing in Jesus's name. Every interview we conducted became less about the testimonies and more about the insights that people had about ministering healing.

James and I did all the filming, I edited and produced the footage, and he wrote and recorded the music. But through the finished product, we creatively produced a film that would (1) present the gospel to anyone who had never heard it, (2) minister healing to viewers, and (3) train and equip Christian viewers to minister healing in Jesus's name to anyone.

In the process of filming, we witnessed more than twenty miracles; and in the decade since, we've seen thousands more.

If you are an apostle, prophet, evangelist, pastor, or teacher, I want to encourage you to consider creative ways of equipping the church. Don't limit yourself to writing or public speaking if you have other talents and skills. Use music or graphic arts. Use film or poetry. And if you do write, don't be afraid to write a fictional story that trains and equips your readers to do what God has called you to do. God can use your creativity to train and equip the church for acts of service.

It's Time to Produce!

Whether you're one God has called to train and equip others, or whether you're privileged to simply carry out the supernatural ministry of Jesus that you've been equipped to do, creativity can produce meaningful results. Be open to the Holy Spirit inspiring you to design prophetic instruments for him to use. This can be a powerful way for him to tangibly speak destiny into people's lives, encourage them toward worship, equip them for ministry, or bring healing to someone who desperately needs it. You could be the craftsman he uses. Imagine what could happen through your hands!

CHAPTER 9

CREATIVITY AND CHANGING SPIRITUAL ATMOSPHERES

Lawgivers don't shape culture; songwriters, artists, and poets do.

—Ray Hughes

O ne of the beauties of creativity—and consequently, one of the things that makes creative people targets of the enemy—is its ability to change the spiritual atmosphere. I'm not talking about some sort of Eastern mysticism like feng shui. I'm talking about affecting the ways people think and act, helping them practice right thinking, and even silencing evil spirits.

For over a decade of my life, I worked with young children— both as a volunteer and as an educated professional. Early on, I learned how important it is to set up an appropriate physical atmosphere for the kids. For example, visual clutter needs to be kept to a minimum so as not to overstimulate and distract the children. Additionally, I regularly played soft music rather than fast driving beats. Parents often came into my classroom and marveled at how all the kids were playing quietly and calmly.

This may seem as if it's all purely dealing with the natural realm, but that's only because we often miss how interconnected the spiritual and natural realms really are.[19] Just as much as these children's bodies and souls are developing, their spirits are as well. By creating a safe and secure environment, I was helping them better sense the peace of the Lord that I brought with me to the classroom, and I was forbidding a spirit of fear or frustration from easily accessing the children. The mental and emotional conditions of the children could either become access points for the enemy or open doors to the expression of the love of God.

I share all this because children give us an exaggerated look at the sensitivity of our own adult bodies, souls, and spirits. You may have experienced the headache and frustration caused by a flickering florescent light bulb or the smell of harsh chemicals. You may have also experienced the calm of walking into a library, the stress of passing through airport security, or the excitement of entering an amusement park. We're all psychologically affected by our physical environments, which can have emotional and even spiritual ramifications.

---

[19] The Old Testament had no word for "spiritual" because all things—even natural things—were understood to have spiritual value on some level.

Creativity influences the atmosphere. The music played, the artwork displayed, and even the décor of a room can affect the ways people think. And just as much as creativity can influence a person's physical and emotional condition, it can also influence the spiritual realm.

Creativity that Subdues Evil Spirits

> Now the Spirit of the Lord had departed from Saul, and an evil spirit from the Lord tormented him.
>
> Saul's attendants said to him, "See, an evil spirit from God is tormenting you. Let our lord command his servants here to search for someone who can play the lyre. He will play when the evil spirit from God comes on you, and you will feel better." …
>
> Whenever the spirit from God came on Saul, David would take up his lyre and play. Then relief would come to Saul; he would feel better, and the evil spirit would leave him. (1 Samuel 16:14–16, 23)

David's musical skills were a weapon of spiritual warfare. He didn't need to use words to cast out the evil spirit. David simply played the harp, and the demon would go.

I've heard it said that there's no such thing as Christian music, only Christian lyrics. The person saying this was trying to make the point that good music is just good music. According to this argument, instrumental arrangements (like classical music, relaxation music, and the like), which have no lyrics, are spiritually neutral.

But if that's true, what do we do with David's harp playing? For that matter, some tribes in Africa use dancing and drum playing to summon evil spirits to do their bidding. Many missionaries have attested to the reality of these dark spiritual forces and how they really do come at the beckoning of the drums. Would you call that music spiritually neutral even though there aren't any lyrics?

The spiritual value of music has a lot to do with the purpose behind it. Songs with lyrics are easier to figure out. For instance, Christian lyrics tend to glorify God, prophesy, encourage, uplift, share the gospel, wage spiritual warfare, or express a prayer. Clearly, we would call all these things good.

On the other side is what we would call secular music, which often has a purpose of mere entertainment. Depending on the mindset it produces in us, we may find ourselves vulnerable to a spirit of depression, lust, greed, fear, anger, discord, or any number of things that don't belong in our lives. Secular music—no matter how fun or wonderful it may seem—often focuses the mind on earthly things, which is contrary to the Word of God. As Colossians 3:2 teaches us, "Set your minds on things above, not on earthly things."

With that said, some secular music does help us think about "whatever is noble … right … pure … lovely … admirable …

excellent or praiseworthy" (Philippians 4:8). In these situations, even secular music can be beneficial to the Christian life.

As the body of Christ, we have a responsibility to set our own minds on things above and to direct the minds of others toward the same heavenly reality. Evidently, David's harp playing would give King Saul a taste of heaven. Jesus said, "If I drive out demons by the finger of God, then the kingdom of God has come upon you" (Luke 11:20). The fact that David's music drove out a demon is proof that Saul encountered God's kingdom. David apparently had his mind set on a heavenly reality, and when he played the harp, the beauty and peace of God's kingdom was expressed, causing demons to flee.

This is true of more than just music. As an artist, writer, musician, inventor, dancer, singer, chef, potter, programmer, decorator, businessperson, or otherwise creative person, you have a powerful ability to bring people into contact with the kingdom of God in tangible ways. Your means of expression do not need to be overtly Christian—again, David's music does not appear to have had any lyrics. All you need to do is set your mind on things above and then engage in the creative process with love for God. The result will be that—like the craftsmen of Israel who built the tabernacle—you will access the pattern of things in heaven and naturally reveal them in the earth.

Creativity and the Glory of God

The book of 2 Chronicles gives us a powerful picture of creativity paving the way for a shift in the spiritual atmosphere. In the first chapter, we find the famous conversation where King Solomon asks God for wisdom. And what is the first kingly act of Solomon after he receives this wisdom from God? Throughout the second chapter, Solomon engages in the creative process, commissioning workers and asking for very specific materials with which to build a temple for the Lord.

Chapters 3 and 4 then detail the creative designs and structures used to build the temple. Solomon's creativity was an expression of wisdom. His mind was set on things above. Everything he did in constructing the temple was with the purpose of worshipping and honoring the Lord. As he directed the work with wisdom, Solomon brought the beauty of heaven to earth in a tangible form.

The supernatural results came in the fifth chapter, where we see further expressions of creativity leading up to a visible shift in the spiritual atmosphere.

> The trumpeters and musicians joined in unison to give praise and thanks to the LORD. Accompanied by trumpets, cymbals and other instruments, the singers raised their voices in praise to the LORD and sang: "He is good; his love endures forever."

Then the temple of the LORD was filled with the cloud, and the priests could not perform their service because of the cloud, for the glory of the LORD filled the temple of God. (2 Chronicles 5:13–14)

Craftsmanship, music, and singing set the stage for a visitation of God's tangible, visible glory in Israel. I don't see any indication that this visitation would have happened apart from these men creatively seeking God—after all, how could God fill the temple if there were no temple? And this spiritual reality had a physical impact on the priests who were present. They were at the mercy of God's presence—unable to engage in earthly duties and held captive to witnessing God.

Dream with Me for a Moment …

What is your form of creativity? No matter what it is—no matter how obscure—it has a role in changing the spiritual atmosphere. The songs you play or sing, the paintings you produce, the words you write, the food you prepare, the dances you perform, the websites you design, the devices you invent, the software you write, the businesses you pioneer, and whatever other ways you engage in the creative process all have the innate capacity for manifesting the kingdom of God. All forms of creativity have the capacity to bring heavenly realities to earth.

Let's make this practical. What could you do creatively in your home to invite the presence of God? How could you influence the atmosphere in such a way that your family has less stress, your friends feel at peace, and everyone who comes through your door senses God's presence?

My wife and I sometimes play worship music throughout the day. We have Scripture-based artwork throughout our house. We have pictures of family, illustrating our love for each other and our honor of previous generations. We have a framed poster from Evangelist Reinhard Bonnke's ministry depicting a massive crowd that gathered to hear the gospel in Africa. We make Jesus the priority of our home, and visitors often remark on the peace they sense or the tangibility of God's presence. Many have been saved, healed, delivered from demons, baptized in water or the Holy Spirit, and more in our home. It has become a place where lives change for the better.

Part of this process has to do with the creativity you personally express in worship to God, and part of it has to do with the worshipful creativity of others that you display in your home.

Think about the creativity you currently welcome into your home. What TV shows do you watch? What books are on your shelves? What music do you listen to? What sort of artwork is displayed? What movies are in your collection? Examine these things. Are they more likely to set your mind on things above? Or are they more likely to set your mind on earthly things?

Over a decade ago, my wife and I decided to give up our cable television. I realized, "Why am I paying somebody money to distract me from Jesus?" A few months later, we gave away our big-screen TV altogether. Without TV, my wife and I discovered how much more time we had for our family, how much more productive we were, and how much less we were influenced by the mindsets of this world.

I'm not saying it's impossible for a Christian to watch TV in a healthy way, but I will say that it's very difficult to "set your mind on things above, not on earthly things" when you're investing an hour or more of your attention (and often your emotions) into worldly entertainment. If you can do it, then I'm happy for you, but we couldn't. The presence and priority of Jesus must become more important to us than our entertainment.

Now let me take you one step further. In love, consider others. Whereas something might really minister to you, it might trouble the conscience of others. I can think of several movies that have become popular in some Christian circles because of the ways Jesus can be seen allegorically in the stories; but many of these movies also include foul language, violence, fallen sexuality, and so forth. Just because those things don't bother you doesn't mean they won't trouble the conscience of someone who enters your home. If we truly love others, then we will be willing to give up our favorite movies, songs, pictures, and so forth for their sake. Just as we should develop an atmosphere that helps set our own minds on things above, we should develop an atmosphere that also sets the minds of others on things above.

The Bible has a lot to say about the importance of leading others in the right direction. Jesus said that it would be better to have a big rock tied around your neck and be drowned in the sea than for you to lead someone into sin. (See Luke 17:2.) And Paul was clear that we should all abstain from anything that would trouble the conscience of another believer. (See 1 Corinthians 8:9–13.) To apply this to our topic, think about the creativity expressed or displayed in your home. Does it set your guests' minds on things above? Or does it keep them trapped in thinking about earthly things? The greatest in the kingdom is the servant of all. Do your choices serve others, or do they serve your own pleasure?

Now take a step out of your home. Think about how you could apply these principles in your place of business, your church, your yard, your neighborhood, and so forth. Suddenly, it becomes apparent how powerful creativity can be at influencing the world around us. Not only do varying media have a psychological impact (like the color of the walls in my preschool class), but they also have a spiritual impact (like the harp music David played for King Saul).

To truly apply everything in this chapter, spend some time meditating on the realities of God's presence. Fix the eyes of your heart on Jesus. Set your mind on things above. Then, as you tune into the realities of heaven, take a look at the world around you. What needs to change in order to reflect the atmosphere of heaven? What would shift the attention of people away from earthly things and help them to think—if only for a moment—about the awesomeness of God? As you spend time with the

Creator, you will gain a clearer perspective of the changes he wants to make in the world around you.

CHAPTER 10

SPENDING TIME
WITH THE CREATOR

Creativity, particularly Spirit-born creativity, is not an end in itself.
Instead, it is a by-product of a relationship with the Creator of the universe.
Creativity is born from the union of the human heart and the divine heart.

—Mark Virkler

*I*n the Jewish culture of the Bible, when a young man reached the onset of puberty (or at thirteen years old), he was considered a full-fledged adult, able to marry, own property, conduct business, and more. The term *bar mitzvah* means "of the commandment" because he has lost his status as a minor and was now expected to keep all the commandments of the Torah.[20]

---

[20] "Bar Mitzvah," *The Bar Mitzvah Book*, ed. Moira Paterson (London: Praeger Publications, 1975).

Conducting business as a thirteen-year-old sounds strange today. If you remember what it was like to be a teenager or if you have teenagers, you might be wondering if this was wise. Adults sometimes think of teenagers as brain-damaged risk-takers with untamable hormones. But biology hasn't really changed in the last few millennia—only our perspectives and expectations have.

What we don't often think about is that the newly dubbed man spent his childhood working alongside his father, learning the family trade. Jesus, for instance, would have helped Joseph prepare wood, draw plans, and expertly craft tools and structures. By the time Jesus was considered a man (at the ripe old age of thirteen), he probably already had more hands-on experience and insight about carpentry than someone today who may have only attended trade school.

By spending time with their fathers, the young men of Israel learned to run their family businesses. Craftsmanship and skill were taught, handed down, and developed.

Our heavenly Father has a family business as well. He is a Creator who deals in acts of love and power. If he can't make something with the available elements, he simply speaks new elements into existence. He is so creative that he thinks outside the realm of what exists. He speaks things that are not as though they are (Romans 4:17). He dreams, he invents, he forms, and he empowers. Our Father's business can be summed up as "limitless, love-filled creativity in action."

How do we become involved in the family business? The same way the young men of the Bible did. We spend time with our Father. We study his craft by watching him at work. We learn from the projects he has done in the past. We ask for insight about the projects that now need to be done. We pay attention and learn from present-day demonstrations of his work. In this way, we learn the family business so that, like Jesus, God can declare over us, "This is my beloved son, in whom I am well pleased," thus commissioning us into the family business. (See Matthew 3:17.)

The more time we spend with our Father, the more his passion takes root in our own hearts, transforming us into trustworthy stewards of his empowered creativity. The more his passion takes root, the more we can express him clearly and powerfully in this world. This starts with a threefold focus on his nature, his works, and his guidance.

1) Focus on His Nature

Some artists will describe the thinking process behind their work. They'll tell you how to bring emotion to your design. Some may even suggest what emotions work best for certain projects. But the more eccentric a creative person is, the less they seem to talk about technique and the more they talk about feeling and color and life.

Similarly, our awesomely creative God spends a lot more time teaching us how to think and live than he spends teaching us how to apply certain techniques. That's because God's creativity is not first about technique. It's about his nature. We are not merely invited to study his methods and strive to perfect them. Rather, we are invited to participate in his nature. As 2 Peter 1:4 says, "Through [God's glory and goodness] he has given us his very great and precious promises, so that through them you may participate in the divine nature and escape the corruption in the world caused by evil desires" (words added for context).

You have been welcomed into participation in God's nature. The more of his nature to which you surrender yourself, the more accurately you can express and convey him. Creativity is part of the package; so as we embrace and acquire his nature, we find a greater capacity to dream like God and think beyond the realm of known possibility.

Therefore, study his nature. Read the Scriptures and focus on the identity of Christ. Recognize who he is in all his majesty. The result is that you'll discover who he has made you to be.

James taught us that when we hear the word of God, it's as though we're looking in a mirror; but if we live differently than the Word reveals, then we have forgotten what we look like. (See James 1:22–24.) In other words, God's Word doesn't give you a list of rules to follow; rather, it tells you what you look like to the Father. You are clothed with Christ, and you share in his identity. As you study the nature of Jesus, you discover who you have been made to be through the power of the Holy Spirit. As Paul said, "I no longer live, but Christ lives in me." (See Galatians 2:20.) You are a new creation, made in the image of God.

Let's make this practical. Jesus is—among other things—creative. Therefore, you are creative. Jesus is victorious over sin; therefore, you are victorious over sin. Jesus is wise and compassionate; therefore, you are wise and compassionate. When you believe in him, he gives you his identity.

My refrigerator is called a "refrigerat-or" because it refrigerates things. Its name is descriptive of what it does. And yet, when that refrigerator rolled off the assembly line at the factory, it was still called a "refrigerator" even though it had never refrigerated anything. It is given the name "refrigerator" not because of what it has done but because of the purpose for which it was made.

Do you see the analogy? God calls you obedient—not because of anything you have or haven't done, but because that's what he made you to be. (See Romans 5:19.) You were given Christ's identity by grace when he made you into a new creation.

You're a "refrigerator" even if you've never refrigerated anything! You're called according to your purpose, not according to your actions. When you read the Bible or hear a prophetic word, you are being told what you look like to the Father. To live any differently is to forget what you look like.

It is natural for a refrigerator to refrigerate things, and it is unnatural for a refrigerator to cook things. If my refrigerator started cooking things, I would either have it fixed or throw it away. That would be against its nature and contrary to its purpose.

Do you see that it is similarly natural for you to live according to the nature of Jesus? You've been made in his image, and now it is natural for you to bear good fruit. Trees don't bear fruit by striving; they bear fruit by being trees. When God tells you who you are, it liberates you to go and be that person.

When you come to Jesus, you instantly look like Jesus to the Father. But you and I both know that we don't always look like Jesus to the people around us. In these moments when we fall short of our identities in Christ, the real culprit is that we've forgotten what we look like. We've forgotten our purpose. We've forgotten our identity. The solution is not to strive. The solution is to be. A warm refrigerator is fixed by plugging it in. An un-Christ-like Christ-follower is fixed by connecting again with the person of Christ through the power of his Holy Spirit. We allow God to trim away whatever is in us that doesn't look like Jesus so that he can be seen more clearly. We continually surrender our flesh to the cross so that the Holy Spirit can reveal Jesus through us.

You can be proactive about your transformation. Each time you discover something that is true of Jesus, realize that it is true of you as well (with the exception that you aren't the Messiah or an eternally existent part of God). When you see that it's true of you, ask yourself whether you actually believe it. And if you believe it, is it being revealed in your life? If it is not being revealed in your life, then why? Do you simply not want to allow Jesus to shine in that way? Do you prefer to gratify your sinful nature? Are you believing that the hurts and experiences of your past have more authority over your actions and identity that Jesus does?

Realize what you look like, and then remember what you look like. This can only be done as we study the nature of Jesus and come to know him in fuller ways. The perfect life of Christ within you will gradually be revealed more and more through you. At some point, people will begin to see more of Jesus than they see of you, and this will shine through in your creativity as well. Your creative expressions will be Christ-centered and focused on his glory. And when God sees one of his children shining his nature and seeking to reveal it to others, he comes alongside to empower the work.

When we focus on the nature of God and respond appropriately, our creative expressions take on a whole new look and feel. We begin to participate in the nature of our Creator. We start to think, act, feel, and live like our Father. When the world sees us, we remind them of our Dad. When our Creator creates, his nature is revealed (Romans 1:20). Whose nature is revealed when you create something?

2) Focus on His Works

As a web developer and graphic designer myself, I have acquired an eye for subtle nuances in the designs made by people I know. Certain friends of mine (myself included) have favorite colors, fonts, and styles. By simply looking at a set of graphics, I can usually tell which of my friends put that design together.

I have found, though, that as I study the works of other designers, my own work begins to take on a different look and feel. It starts to reflect the creative eye of those I admire.

When we learn how to apply our creativity from a seasoned veteran, we start to pick up on that person's favorites. Their style is intermingled with ours, resulting in the development of something completely new. Our works begin to look more and more like the works of those we admire most.

Who do you admire most? Is it someone on this planet? Is it the enemy? Is it yourself? Or is it Jesus?

If the focus of your admiration is the works of mere men, then your talent may improve, but you will have a hard time producing works of supernatural value. I'm not saying that you never will; I'm just saying that all things reproduce after their own kind. If you only study the works of man, you will become very successful at reproducing quality works of man. You should work at and pursue increasing earthly skill but not at the expense of making Christ your primary tutor.

Likewise, if your focus is on the enemy, then you won't produce anything truly creative. Your works will rather be destructive and contrary to the kingdom. What entertainment do you choose? What strongholds are you building in your mind? These will multiply in your creativity.

And if your focus is on yourself, then you will stagnate in your craft, never moving too far beyond what you have already accomplished. Pride is a killer in more ways than one.

But if your focus is on Christ, then there are no limits to what you can learn. Study his works, and you'll probably find yourself struggling to keep up with all the creative thoughts and ideas that flow from following his example.

You may have figured out by now that I'm not specifically referring to examples of craftsmanship and design during the ministry of Christ. On the contrary, I'm talking about two things: (1) the physical creation all around us and (2) the supernatural demonstrations of God's love and power throughout the Bible, history, and the present day.

As we study the works of Jesus—his power to forgive, heal, raise the dead, cast out demons, prophesy, and so forth—we discover the power-packed potential of the Christian life. And as we apply God's creative nature to this discovery, we find ourselves designing creations with spiritual value. Like Moses's bronze snake, Ezekiel's model of Jerusalem, and David's harp playing, our creative expressions begin to heal the sick, prophesy, and cast out demons in the name of Jesus. Our works begin to take on the traits of his works.

Nevertheless, observing his works on their own is not enough. The purpose of studying his works is to learn his ways.

When I study the graphic designs and web designs of people I admire, I'm constantly thinking, "How did they do that?" If I can describe their work but can't replicate it, then I haven't really benefited from my study. The purpose of studying an artist's work is to learn how to apply that artist's principles and techniques to your own work.

David indicated that God made his works known to the people of Israel, but Moses had the privilege of discovering his ways (Psalm 103:7). The Israelites knew that God was powerful, but they didn't have a relationship with him. They constantly asked Moses to speak to him on their behalf. The people enjoyed seeing all manner of miracles—from the plagues of Egypt to the parting of the Red Sea to supernatural provision of food and water—but they were not students of those miracles. They did not learn God's ways. Moses, on the other hand, spent extended time with God, meeting with him face to face. Moses learned from God's works and—through intimacy with the Lord—discovered his ways. This did not result in an ability to manipulate God. Rather, it resulted in an understanding of God's will and a capacity to reveal that will through acts of power.

We, too, should become students of the works of God—not merely experiencing his power but seeking to comprehend him as a Person. The better our understanding of the ways of God, the better we will be able to wield the weapon of empowered creativity according to his will.

3) Focus on His Guidance

As a young Hebrew boy learned his father's trade, the father would naturally need to give him hands-on opportunities to succeed or fail. Along the way, the Father would have the responsibility to encourage and correct, helping the boy to hone his skills and better reflect the father's vision.

As we engage in the creative process, we need to be open to the Lord's guidance as he brings correction or encouragement. He will show us how we could have done things better. His purpose is not to make us feel inept but to make us better stewards of the family business.

When I first started practicing the gift of prophecy, I would run to God like a little kid after a school performance runs to his own dad. "How did I do?" I would ask. Then, naturally, my heavenly Father would both encourage me and gently point out where I allowed my flesh to get in the way and how I could have conveyed his point better. I didn't let the correction beat me down though. Rather, I applied what I learned the next time, knowing that God approved of me even if I made mistakes. Sometimes I'd hit the nail on the head, and other times, he would have more correction for me. If I never asked for his guidance, then I wouldn't be a very good steward of his work.

As a writer, I often encounter what many call writer's block—I find myself unable to write anything more and feel completely uninspired. The world will teach you that the best thing you can do when you have writer's block is simply to write. For earthly writing, I suppose that has some value. But I know that what I write is for the purposes of the kingdom and has the potential to make or break a person's spiritual walk in a given area. I recognize the weightiness of my mission and the gravity of my craft. What I've learned is that—at least for me—writer's block is God's way of telling me that either something is missing in my presentation or that I've written something that needs to be corrected.

This very book, which took me ten years to compile, sat untouched on the hard drive of my computer for two whole years before I sensed the Lord guide me back to it, and then it sat untouched for six more years. I finished the original manuscript in 2012 but couldn't shake the feeling that it wasn't yet ready to be published. I entered a contract with a well-known Christian publisher before I even wrote the book, so I already had a publisher. I simply knew in my spirit that something wasn't right.

Four years later, I started at page one and began to read through the book I had written. I found so many things I had written that God has corrected me on during the previous couple of years. I was teaching on subjects that could have produced performance-driven behavior instead of an understanding of grace and identity. The Holy Spirit constrained me from publishing a book that could have put people in bondage so that I could present a better message of freedom in Christ.

And most recently, I sensed God's grace on the project yet again. I again worked through the book from the beginning and polished it with stronger writing skills, better examples, and more refined theology. Additionally, my graphic design skills have improved to a point where I could make the cover and pages of the printed book look great. About five years ago, I asked to be released from the contract with the big publishing company because I now operated my own publishing company and wanted to release it there. Finally, the book was ready for editing, printing, and release.

I have often found that writer's block is an invitation to revisit what I have already written and discover what the Lord wants to improve or change. I try not to write without a feeling of inspiration. Some of my books were produced in a matter of thirty days or less, but others, like this one, are long-term projects that the Lord is helping me sharpen before their release.

God desires for our works to be Christ-centered, love-filled, and saturated with power through the Holy Spirit. He wants his children to effectively transform this world. He wants our works to be extensions of his own work, bringing destruction to the works of the devil (1 John 3:8).

To accomplish this, God will help guide us toward a pure expression of his righteous will—one that is not too terribly muddied by our occasional fleshly shortcomings. We may never reach the full magnitude of that goal, but it's a life worth seeking. Let the Lord correct and train you as you learn his ways and embrace his nature.

Learn to Think like Dad

The outcome of this threefold focus is not to simply cause us to mimic our Father. In the natural realm, we know that it isn't healthy for young people to be obligated to always dress, speak, and behave exactly like their earthly dads. This robs them of their own individuality. However, it is healthy for them to embrace whatever godly wisdom and lifestyle their father might pass down.

As much as the Scripture calls us to represent Christ and reveal him through participating in his nature, we are also called to fulfill unique roles in his body, the church. Remember, we are all one body made up of many parts. We have different ways of expressing and revealing Christ. We are each a necessary puzzle piece in the grand revelation of Jesus in this world. As such, we are called to live in unity so that together we can reveal the fullness of our heavenly Dad.

I can walk because my right leg and left leg work in harmony. They don't do the same exact thing—otherwise, I'd be exhausted from jumping everywhere I go, and I'd probably fall down a lot. Neither do my legs act independently—otherwise, I'd probably inadvertently kick everyone around me. No, my right and left legs each receive instruction from my brain about how to move and where to take me. They are unique, but they are in unity.

All the parts of my body are in unity with each other because of one simple fact: They all receive their instructions from my brain. When my brain wants to do something, my body responds appropriately.

In the same way, we are designed to be uniquely unified. We aren't all called to be heads. Christ is our head. And we don't have to be like everyone else. We simply need to be in unity with Jesus by learning to think like him and embracing the promptings of his Spirit within us.

Thus, we become the hands and feet of Christ. Everything we do becomes an extension of him. People can see Jesus in our every word and action when we live wholly surrendered to his will. The head directs the body, so learn to think like Jesus. Every believer has the mind of Christ (1 Corinthians 2:16). It's natural to think like Jesus when his Spirit lives in you.

Spend time with the Creator. Let him father you and teach you his ways. Learn from his nature and his works. Let him guide you and refine your life. In time, your unity with Christ will be strengthened, and you will begin to think like your Father in new ways.

Jesus only did what he saw his Father doing, and we, too, can receive such a revelation of the Father's present work that we can't help but join him. (See John 5:19.) Let him empower your creativity.

CHAPTER 11

LIMITLESS, LOVE-FILLED CREATIVITY IN ACTION

Whatever God's dream about man may be,
it seems certain it cannot come true unless man cooperates.
—Stella Terrill Mann

At the beginning of the previous chapter, I suggested that our Father's family business could be summed up as "limitless, love-filled creativity in action." In this chapter, I want to explain each of these descriptive terms so that you can see how to implement them in your own creative expressions. Consider this chapter a manual on how to carry on the family business.

Limitless Creativity

In the world, creativity always has limits. King Solomon observed, "There is nothing new under the sun" (Ecclesiastes 1:9). This earth is considered "under the sun," but God holds the universe in the palm of his hand. While the world fails to produce anything truly new, God says, "Behold, I am doing a new thing" (Isaiah 43:19). Every time someone comes to Christ, God jumps back into the creative process to make something that no one has seen before. "Therefore, if anyone is in Christ, he is a new creation; the old has gone, the new has come!" (2 Corinthians 5:17).

God has established limits on the world's creativity for a purpose, and we receive a glimpse of that purpose early in the Bible. Only a few generations after Noah's flood, all the people of the world lived in one place. Then we find this story:

> They began saying to each other, "Let's make bricks and harden them with fire." (In this region bricks were used instead of stone, and tar was used for mortar.) Then they said, "Come, let's build a great city for ourselves with a tower that reaches into the sky. This will make us famous and keep us from being scattered all over the world."
>
> But the Lord came down to look at the city and the tower the people were building. "Look!" he said. "The people are united, and they all speak the same language. After this, nothing they set out to do will be impossible for them! Come, let's go down and confuse the people

with different languages. Then they won't be able to understand each other." (Genesis 11:3–7 NLT)

Some have wondered why God would stop people from accomplishing something so wonderful. The people seemed to want to live in unity with each other. Doesn't God want us to do the impossible? Why would he stop these people?

The issue is that the people were capable of doing the impossible apart from God. They had the capacity to thrive without his intervention. If God hadn't limited their creative potential, he could have easily been lost to history as the human race moved on and failed to acknowledge him.

But God—in his love for all humanity throughout time—knew that this would ultimately lead to eternal destruction for all people. He knew that in order to bring about a transformation of all things in Christ, people would need to need him. So he limited their creativity. He scattered them, and mankind could no longer do the impossible apart from Christ. In the world, creativity has limits so that we will still reach out to God when all our efforts fail.

In Christ, however, creativity has no limits because it is empowered by our limitless God. Empowered creativity can influence every single medium without limit. While the world takes time to make wine out of grapes, Jesus instantly makes better wine out of mere water.

Jesus has the market cornered on the impossible. That which is possible, he has entrusted to mankind to discover; but that which is impossible, he has entrusted only to the church. As Deuteronomy 29:29 says, "The secret things belong to the Lord our God, but the things revealed belong to us and to our children forever."

Jesus didn't invent the hearing aid. He didn't come down from heaven and teach people how to perform outpatient surgeries. He didn't start a business of training seeing-eye-dogs. He didn't even come with a message of good nutrition or proper exercise. Nope. He came giving sight to the blind, opening deaf ears, healing the paralytic, and telling his disciples, "Even if you drink deadly poison, it won't harm you!" (See Mark 16:18.)

Ultimately, all wisdom and knowledge come from Christ. Colossians 2:3 says that "in Christ are hidden all the treasures of wisdom and knowledge." So Jesus, knowing everything there is to know, could have left heaven with blueprints for the X-ray machine or information about penicillin. But he didn't.

Think about that: Jesus, who was present at creation, didn't come to teach mankind things that we could discover on our own. He came to do the impossible.

We can glean a few things from this: First, Jesus came to reveal a God of the impossible. Second, God wants to use our creativity rather than merely tell us how to do things. And third, as we partner with him, Jesus intends for our creativity to function in the realm of impossibilities.

God invites us to invent what is possible for us to invent. Jesus didn't come to advance technology—that's for us to enjoy.

But he has also given his church the liberty to think outside the box. If indeed we are partnering with Christ in his creativity, then we have the same infinite resources of the Holy Spirit's power backing us up.

Our Lord prefers heart transformation over heart transplants. He prefers renewing the mind over brain surgery. And he prefers resurrection over CPR. (Jesus threw a monkey-wrench in every funeral he ever attended, regularly raising the dead.) Jesus came to establish a kingdom, not a hospital.

Now, is this to discredit all the wonderful advances that we've made in medicine and technology? Not at all. Remember, God is pleased to allow mankind to be creative—especially if it's helping people live longer so that they have more time to accept him (or more time to impact others because they've already accepted him).

God invites all mankind to reveal his creative nature, but the impossible is off-limits to those who do not know him. This is an exciting thought, because it means the opposite is also true: To those who do know God, the impossible is our inheritance! Limitless creativity is the family business.

When I was filming *Paid in Full*, one of my interview subjects told me about a church meeting he once attended. A professional baker also attended the meeting and brought a large cake. He said, "God told me this morning that everyone who eats this cake today will be healed." That's a bold claim, but that's what happened. While not every condition could be immediately tested, I'm told that everyone who could verify a positive change confirmed this. Everyone said they were healed as they ate the cake.

No ordinary person can make a cake that heals the sick. But a Spirit-filled believer can make a cake in faith, and God can use it to accomplish the impossible.

If you want to be like Jesus, don't settle for natural abilities. As Jesus put it, "What is impossible with men is possible with God" (Luke 18:27). Feel free to design earthly inventions and so forth, but don't lock yourself into that which is considered possible. Reach for the impossible! Create with spiritual significance. A bronze snake that heals snakebite victims is impossible. A temple that fills with smoke from heaven is impossible. An instrumental solo that expels demons is impossible. Create with a kingdom purpose and help advance the cause of righteousness in this world.

Love-Filled Creativity

The purpose of creativity is to reveal our Creator. True creativity, then, gives the world an opportunity to encounter God. Without love, though, our efforts are useless.

As you've seen throughout this book, spiritual gifts and creativity go hand in hand. So it only makes sense that we should be able to learn from what Paul said about love as it relates to spiritual gifts.

If I speak in the tongues of men or of angels, but do not have love, I am only a resounding gong or a clanging cymbal. If I have the gift of prophecy and can fathom all mysteries and all knowledge, and if I have a faith that can move mountains, but do not have love, I am nothing. If I give all I possess to the poor and give over my body to hardship that I may boast, but do not have love, I gain nothing. (1 Corinthians 13:1–3)

Likewise, if I make a sculpture that heals the sick but don't have love, I am nothing. If I paint a prophecy with perfect artistry but don't have love, I'm nothing. If I can write and perform songs that dispel demons but don't have love, I'm nothing. If I can make plain the mysteries of God through drama, public speaking, or writing, but don't have love, I'm nothing. Without love, I'm missing the point. Love is the necessary context for the supernatural to truly convey God's heart.

Interestingly, in Paul's words, he doesn't say that the prophecy, the tongues, the knowledge, the faith, the giving, or the endurance are nothing. He said that he himself would be nothing. So it's good if you design something that reveals God, but without love, you fall short of your purpose and identity.

You see, God could have used wind and water erosion to make a sculpture without you. He could use the charred pattern on a grilled-cheese sandwich to sketch a picture (just ask eBay). He could have made the birds sing the song you wrote or the trees perform your dance. Jesus told us that if we don't praise him, the rocks will cry out (Luke 19:40). God could arrive at the same results without using a human being—and he might even do a better job. But what wind, water, fire, birds, trees, and rocks cannot do is express his love. That's why God uses people to produce these spiritual weapons. People have a capacity for love. Since we are the best representatives of his nature to the world, we are the best candidates for doing his works.

This is why it is so important that we love. If we don't love, then God might as well use the inanimate forces of nature to accomplish the same results. If we don't love, we're nothing. But if we do love, then we are doing something that no other aspect of nature can do. We are revealing more than a message or a concept. We are revealing a Person. Our artistry reveals God in a visible, audible, or tangible way; but our love reveals him in a meaningful way.

Paul's letter to the Roman church makes it painfully clear that God's use of creation to reveal himself, while adequate, has not been effective at drawing all the world to himself.

> The wrath of God is being revealed from heaven against all the godlessness and wickedness of people, who suppress the truth by their wickedness, since what may be known about God is plain to them, because God has made it plain to them. For since the creation of the world God's invisible qualities—his eternal power and divine nature—

have been clearly seen, being understood from what has been made, so that people are without excuse....

They exchanged the truth about God for a lie, and worshiped and served created things rather than the Creator—who is forever praised. Amen. (Romans 1:18–20, 25)

Creation is not enough. Love is the missing component. I'm not saying that God doesn't love us through his creation, because he most definitely does. But the world—for the most part—has not understood that love. Although creation reveals the attributes of God, it is nevertheless impersonal and lacking a face. To meet this need, God has enlisted people like you and me to love the world in practical ways, bringing light to the reality of his passion for mankind. You put a face on his love. God is love, and you bear his image (1 John 4:7–8). God empowers your creativity because you have the advantage of loving people face to face. He wants you to do more than make creative works. He wants you to love.

In 1 Corinthians 14:1, Paul encouraged us to "desire spiritual gifts" (NKJV). But in that same verse, he also instructed us to "pursue love." Gifts are desired while love is pursued. The difference between desire and pursuit is that one is easy and the other takes effort. As you desire spiritual gifts, you naturally take action to operate in those gifts and create opportunities for God to work them in your life. That's easy because it takes very little self-sacrifice to accomplish, and it's motivated by your desire. But love must be pursued. Love requires significant self-sacrifice, and that isn't always easy. It's natural, but not easy.

Desire is emotion-based, and pursuit is decision-based. A police officer does not have to enjoy a car chase. If a criminal needs to be pursued, then the officer needs to follow—regardless of how he feels. In the same way, we can easily desire spiritual gifts because they are exciting. But love is not a mere emotion. Love is a decisive action of purposeful self-sacrifice.

This is the type of creativity to which we are called. Everything God created was done in love. In fact, he is love. He decisively self-sacrificed, risking his heart to us by granting us free will. In the same way, we must pursue love. We must go out of our way to look for creative ways to love people.

As we engage in the creative process, we should be asking, "What can I do to more effectively love people with what I'm making?" The answer may require that you be inconvenienced. It may require a loss of income. It may require a more difficult method or technique. But love demands that we consider others more highly than ourselves. Our responsibility is not to promote ourselves—that's God's responsibility. Our responsibility is simply to love selflessly with humility and joy.

...In Action!

For much of my young life, I was great at being creative and coming up with all manner of outside-the-box, grandiose ideas. But I never implemented them. Part of the problem was that I didn't have the resources at the time to do what I wanted to do. Another part of the problem was that I didn't have the influence to do what I wanted to do. And yet another part is that I'm a dreamer by nature, and I often need people around me to put feet to many of my ideas.

Creativity without action is just as meaningless as faith without action. You can be a very creative person; but if you never put that creativity to work, then it only serves your ego. No one else benefits. Ideas are nice, but action brings such ideas to life.

Our Father has not been sitting around for all eternity, merely thinking about creation. Rather, he put his dreams and plans into action with love. Nothing stood in his way. Our incomparable, relentless God put limitless, love-filled creativity into action purely for our sake; and he did not rest until it was complete.

One could argue that it was easy for him. He has all power, and he merely spoke all creation into existence. But creation still came with a tremendous sacrifice. God risked his heart to us, investing himself in mankind and giving us the free will to reject him and trample on his love. He knew it would happen, so he set aside Christ from the very foundations of the world to pay the price for our redemption (Revelation 13:8). While creating the universe was easy for God, it was not without great cost.

Creativity always comes with a price tag. There will always be a cost. But like an artist who sells his work, the return is usually far greater than the investment. Just as Jesus received a far greater reward than the price of his own suffering—the salvation of all who would believe in him—so, too, will we reap more than we sow.

A little bit of music lessons and some time in a studio could result in a song that impacts the world and tears down strongholds. A square of canvas and some paint could speak prophetic destiny to an entire generation of young people. A few words typed into a computer could result in a life-altering book that spurs millions of Christians on toward love and good deeds.

Don't fear the cost. Don't fear the investment of time or the missed opportunities for recreation. Imagine if Noah had that attitude when God told him to build the ark. None of us would be here today. Instead, embrace the cost for the sake of the mission. Jesus endured the cross because of the joy that would result (Hebrews 12:2). You can endure a little bit of inconvenience in order to put limitless, love-filled creativity into action.

CHAPTER 12

UNLEASHING EMPOWERED CREATIVITY

Fan-based Christianity will never have a positive influence
on an ego-driven culture.

—Ray Hughes

*T*he unstoppable potential of empowered creativity makes you dangerous to the kingdom of darkness. As we saw in chapter 7, our enemy specifically targets those of us who enjoy being creative. The apostle Paul commented that we are not unaware of the devil's schemes (2 Corinthians 2:10–11). The context of this statement is that we must forgive the people who have wounded us in our past—otherwise, Satan may have an opportunity to outwit us.

Due to painful experiences, we often carry mindsets and attitudes that can slow us down or even disarm us if left unchecked. These mindsets tend to put restrictions on our creativity. The only restraint that should be on your creativity is the need to focus it on loving and obeying God. With that perspective established, though, the sky's the limit on everything else. You have the liberty to be as creative as you possibly can be (and perhaps even go beyond that) with help from the Holy Spirit.

Establishing the right mindset will unleash your God-given creativity so that you can partner with God in doing the impossible through the guidance and power of the Holy Spirit. Among other things, you will need to deal with negative mindsets, such as performance orientation, pride, independence, greed, selfishness, and apathy. None of these are part of your identity in Christ, so they're easy to solve. We simply need to grant Jesus more authority over our beliefs, thoughts, and actions than we grant to painful experiences or lies from the enemy. The result will be empowered creativity, unleashed.

Performance Orientation

Why do you express your creativity in the ways you do? Is it so you can bring glory to God and allow him to minister to people through you? Is it to attract attention to yourself and please people? Or is it to please God and earn his favor?

Most of us would probably answer with the first reason because it's the right, churchy answer. But churchy answers rarely lead to transformation. Churchy answers are what Christians give by default when we know what's right and want to ignore the fact that we aren't doing it. Churchy answers, interestingly enough, come from the very topic I'm talking about here: performance orientation.[21]

The second two reasons are usually the true motivations behind our actions, and yet neither is healthy. On one side, we find ourselves striving to please mankind, which is of little value in the scope of eternity. On the other side, we find ourselves striving to please a God who is already well pleased with us—not because of our amazing actions or righteous deeds but simply because we know Jesus. Both of these are performance-based motivations and are not based on a true, loving relationship with the Lord.

Performance orientation is one of the most insidious blocks against healthy creativity. If you can escape it, then you'll not only have more fun, but you'll also be far more effective in the spiritual warfare that God wants to wage through your creativity.

Performance orientation can be defined as the inner compulsion to please God, yourself, or others through unhealthy striving. The usual result is perfectionism, which stifles our creativity and can even lock us into inactivity.

I used to be extremely performance-oriented. How bad was it? Well, let me tell you about when I used to work on a farm.

---

[21] I first learned about performance orientation from the writings of John Loren Sandford—specifically, the book *Deliverance and Inner Healing* by him and his son, Mark Sandford. I have found his perspective tested and true, and I want to honor the Sandfords for blazing trails in this area.

One day my boss—who is now my father-in-law—sent me to a horse pasture that needed to be used as a parking lot for an upcoming big event. To clean up for the visitors, all the manure had to be shoveled into wheelbarrows and hauled away. Nearly ten horses, a few donkeys, and a couple of cows all shared this field, so I had plenty to shovel.

My girlfriend's father really liked speedy work, so I zipped through the first quarter-acre. As his truck rolled toward me, I was rather pleased with myself and couldn't wait to hear his words of affirmation.

Instead, he said this: "You're going too fast—there's no way you could have caught everything! Go back and do a better job."

It was a big blow to my ego, but I wanted to perform well to please my future father-in-law. So naturally, I hurried back to the beginning and cleaned up what little I missed.

By the time I was halfway through the pasture, it was nearly time for me to go home for the day. I had perfected my scooping to a science. Not a bit of manure was left, and I was once again rather pleased with myself. One wheelbarrow after the next had been hauled off to a pile at the end of the pasture. Once again, my boss rolled up in his truck. I grew excited—rather proud of myself for my excellence.

"Aren't you done yet? What's taking you so long?" he asked.

I started fuming. My blood rushed to my head, and a flood of frustration washed over me.

"I'm just trying to do a good job for you," I calmly managed to reply.

"Well, it doesn't have to be perfect," he said. "Perfect takes too long and isn't necessary. Just do ninety percent."

That made me even angrier! It wasn't so much that I felt like I had just wasted a lot of time and effort (which was true), but I was mostly bent out of shape about the "ninety percent" instruction. Since I was performance-oriented and a perfectionist, I couldn't handle such an unmeasurable statistic.

How does he expect me to know what "ninety percent" of a pile of manure is? I asked myself. *For that matter, he didn't see the whole pile; so how will he know when I've succeeded? For all I know, he'll just come out here, see the ten percent remaining, and make me clean the pasture all over again!*

Have you ever been there? Have you ever felt like no matter what you did, you just couldn't please someone? How did that make you feel? Were you cool with it? Or did you nearly have a nervous breakdown like I did?

If your reaction was similar to mine, then you might be struggling with performance orientation. If not dealt with, this can severely impair more aspects of your life than just creativity, so I want to offer you the truth that can set you free.

It is quite simple. Sometimes it's as basic as realizing that God is the only one we need to please, and that revelation comes easy when we see that God's pleasure for his children is not based on our performance but the fact that we belong to him. Other times—as in my case—we need to ask the Holy Spirit to reveal the root cause of why we think the way we do.

After that experience on the farm, I chose to deal with my frustration through prayer (always a good idea, by the way). I asked the Holy Spirit to show me what event in my life set me on this course of performance orientation.

Instantly, a memory popped into my mind that I hadn't thought about in years. Even though it had been the last thing on my mind for so long, it somehow felt connected. The memory was of myself as a young child. I had just colored a picture with some crayons and raced to my dad to show him my masterpiece. He looked at it, said, "Very nice, son," and went back to what he was doing. I stood there stunned, the paper trembling in my hands as tears began to run down my cheeks.

"What's the matter?" he asked—completely blindsided by my response. "I said it was nice!"

"I thought you'd be more excited," I whimpered through gasps.

"Well, honey," he replied with compassion, "if I get overly excited about everything you do, then you won't know when you've really done something well."

My dad is one of the greatest men of God I've ever known; and his heart was in the right spot when he said this. But my young, emotional mind translated his words as hurtful. Deep inside, I determined to do everything as perfectly as possible so that people would be really excited about me, rather than only moderately pleased.

I began to only tackle activities that I could quickly excel at. If too much practice or effort were involved, I would bail. As a result, I loved English in school and hated math. English came naturally, but math was a chore and took practice. I discovered— perhaps subconsciously—that if I hated math, then I had a reason to not put much time or effort into it. I passed my math tests, but I never turned in the homework assignments. I was failing in the gradebook but succeeding in my mind. After all, anyone can ace a test after doing all the homework and studying. Isn't it way more amazing to pass it without doing the homework or any other preparation? Even though I wasn't performing well, this was performance orientation, pure and simple.

This spread throughout all my schoolwork. I was never satisfied with projects and writing assignments because they could always be better. But I had peace about deadlines because they established a definite end to my otherwise endless tweaking of schoolwork. As a result, I subconsciously put off projects until the last minute so I didn't have to waste as much time fussing over details.

And that brought me all the way through life until that day on the farm.

The Lord led me through a process of forgiving my dad— even though my dad didn't technically do anything wrong. Then he revealed a few more instances in my life that had reinforced my need to please people and perform, and I walked through the process of forgiveness in those events as well.

Suddenly, I found a depth of personal inner freedom in Christ that I had never known before. I began basing my value and worth on what God says about me rather than on what people around me might think. I stopped letting the expectations of people drive my motivation and simply surrendered to the love of God. I found a release of creativity in my life, unhindered by the inner drive to perform for others. Now my creative expressions were free from compulsion and full of enjoyment—purely for the sake of bringing glory to the God who already loves me.

Do you want this kind of life? Ask the Lord to reveal what past situations may have set you on a course of performance orientation. Allow him to walk you through the process of forgiveness through Christ, and embrace the freedom he gives.

Misunderstood Identity

As exciting as my newfound freedom was, I discovered a new problem. It was as if a pendulum had been released that swung far to the other extreme. Once I was free from performance orientation, my college GPA dropped from a perfect 4.0 to a less impressive 2.8. I even almost failed one class.

I began to panic. Something seemed broken. God had healed my heart, but it seemed to be bearing bad fruit in my life.

I prayed about it, and the Lord said, "You effectively came to the cross, but you're still laying in the tomb."

I had rightly died to my false motivation, forgiving my dad and others for the wounds that had spurred me to perfectionism for so many years. But I never allowed the Lord to awaken a right motivation in me.

He said, "You used to be a perfectionist because you were trying to prove yourself, but I have proved you. Today, you are a new creation. You no longer live. I live in you. Today, you do things with excellence simply because I do things with excellence."

My identity in Christ meant Jesus is alive in me, ready to reveal himself through my yielded participation with him. I no longer had an inner drive to perform, but I do have the Perfect One living in me, and I can trust him to do things well.

I began trusting the Lord to empower me with his nature. The same excellent Student who taught the teachers when he was twelve years old began being an excellent student through me (Luke 2:46–47). I found myself learning better than I previously had. I did my projects with excellence not because of an inner need to prove myself but because Jesus is excellent, and he lives in me. I finished college on the Dean's List with a 3.8 GPA.

When you know who Jesus is, you know who Jesus is in you. He is expressed through faith. That means we trust him to be consistently himself without fail.

I don't worry about whether I'll be a good husband because Jesus is the perfect Bridegroom, and he lives in me. I don't worry about being a good father because the One who perfectly reveals the perfect Father lives in me. I don't worry about sin, failure, or poor performance. And naturally, I don't feel a need to try to be creative. I simply trust the creative One who lives in me to inspire creativity in me.

Pride

One of my biggest issues has always been pride. It's not because pride is part of my identity, because it certainly isn't. Jesus isn't prideful, and he lives in me. But I can easily slip out of a mindset in which my focus is on him and slip into a mindset in which my focus is on myself.

We all battle with pride in one form or another. The trouble is that we often don't recognize it—after all, that's the nature of pride.

I have a friend who once came to me, terrified by a dream he had. He saw all kinds of evil people attacking each other with swords while he watched from up high on a cloud. The most troubling part, he said, was that he could feel the stabbing, slashing, and hacking himself as though he were down there with all those people. He asked, "Do you think this means anything?"

The Lord showed me the interpretation immediately. I answered, "Yes, but I don't know if you really want to know what it means."

After he begged me for a little bit, I gave in and shared the interpretation: "I feel like those people are doing what happened in various biblical stories. At times, God's people won military victories because their enemies turned on each other and killed each other in confusion. What you saw in the dream was the confusion caused by wickedness that leads to destruction."

"That makes sense," he replied. "The people were wicked and fighting each other. I get that. But why was I feeling pain as if I were with them?"

"Because you weren't standing on a cloud, you were standing on a cliff. And the cloud was blinding you to the fact that more of those people were behind you, attacking you. The cloud represents pride, which has made you think that you're somehow higher than all those people; but the reality is that you're one of them."

I didn't really like sharing such a harsh interpretation, but I was glad I did. This young man's response was to repent and dedicate his life to the Lord. Until that time, he was an occasional churchgoer but didn't have any evidence of the Spirit's work in his life. Now, almost twenty years later, he's still growing in his faith and leading his family with more and more humility.

Pride squelches empowered creativity by blinding us to the fact that we're not expressing Jesus. It causes us to think that we're doing the right thing when, in fact, we're promoting our flesh. As a result, our creativity tends to be self-centered. It becomes about exalting ourselves rather than exalting Christ. It becomes about promoting our own names rather than promoting his name.

It's not impossible to exercise humility while still battling pride. The key is that we identify the "cloud" of pride for what it is and choose to live the opposite. Rather than focusing on how wicked everybody else is (which makes us feel better about our "less evil" condition), we focus on how righteous and good Jesus is (which makes us worship him more and serve him with invigorated passion). Humility is a focus on Jesus. Humility is worship. Humility is setting your mind on things above rather than on earthly things.

Can you see now how pride puts a damper on empowered creativity? A heart of humility is an atmosphere ripe for the supernatural power of God. James 4:6 tells us that "God opposes the proud but gives grace to the humble." Humility invites the grace of God; and in the original Greek language of the Bible, the word in this verse for "grace" (*charis*) is very closely related to the word for "gifts" (*charisma*) of the Spirit in 1 Corinthians 12:31.[22] Grace is an enabling force. In other words, grace and power go hand in hand. This is why Peter wrote, "Each of you should use whatever gift you have received to serve others, as faithful stewards of God's grace in its various forms" (1 Peter 4:10).

When Noah built a giant boat in faith, God empowered the results. But when Noah's descendants tried making a giant tower only a few generations later, God opposed it. The boat was built in humility, but the tower was built in pride. One was empowered while the other was opposed. If you want God to empower your creativity, surrender your pride to the cross.

---

[22] "χαρίσματα [*charismata*]," Bible Hub.com, accessed August 30, 2022, https://biblehub.com/greek/charismata_5486.htm.

Independence

Way back in chapter 2, I talked about a set of men who King David commissioned to prophesy with music and song. Interestingly, all these men carried out their ministries within the context of being under authority, according to God's order:

> All these men were under the supervision of their father for the music of the temple of the Lord, with cymbals, lyres and harps, for the ministry at the house of God.
>
> Asaph, Jeduthun and Heman were under the supervision of the king. Along with their relatives—all of them trained and skilled in music for the Lord—they numbered 288. (1 Chronicles 25:6–7)

King David oversaw the three fathers, and the fathers oversaw their sons. We can learn from this today. It's one thing to interrupt a moment of silence by shouting a prophecy (or supposed prophecy) during a church service or event. Anyone can do that. But to stand in front of people with a musical instrument and sing a prophecy probably will only happen if you've been granted the venue by someone with the authority to do so.

Many of us have been wounded by people who improperly wielded authority. Plenty of people in the world have misused their positions of influence for personal gratification. But that doesn't mean God doesn't grant some people positions of authority in the church.

The present subject does not allow for a discussion about what types of authority are healthy and biblical versus what types are inventions of man. We all know authority can be misused. My focus here is on how we can humbly partner with people of influence and thereby gain a greater audience than we would have had on our own.

My advice to creative people who want to exercise their spiritual and prophetic gifts publicly is this: Submit to authority. Whether we're talking about healthy authority or unhealthy authority, the way to such a person's heart is the same. God wants to use you to sing his heart to his people and stir their souls. He wants your prophetic artwork to be displayed. He wants your programs to be implemented and your books to be promoted. He wants your expression of him to have an audience who will experience the ministry he intends. I have learned from experience that the best way to gain an audience is through humility and submission.

When my wife, Robin, and I became engaged, the Holy Spirit led me to leave the church I was attending (which I had helped plant four years earlier) and attend her church. I set up an appointment with the pastor to introduce myself. "Hi Pastor Brooks," I started, "I just wanted to come by and let you know that I'll be attending your church. I also wanted to know if there is any way I can help you fulfill your vision."

"Well," he replied, "what are your passions?"

I told him about my love for young adult ministry and older teens. I told him about my experience and education in Early Childhood Development. Two months later, I was officially part of the staff as an assistant pastor of student ministries in a relatively large church of several hundred people.

I didn't have any ministerial credentials at the time—those came a year after I was hired. And I didn't get the job because I wowed the senior pastor with my talents and skills. Rather, I was given a voice of influence simply because of the favor of the Lord and my genuine desire to serve someone who had authority. Influence in ministry comes through submission to others and the heart of a servant.

This is a completely different perspective for most musicians and artists. Our culture has taught us that if you want to go places with your talent, then you have to put on a show. You have to be the star and perform with blind confidence. In other words, you have to raise yourself up.

That's called pride, by the way.

Prophetic singers and musicians (among other creative expressions), however, can only rise to prominence through humility and submission to authority. That's how they receive their platforms. That's how they're granted an audience with kings.

> Do not exalt yourself in the king's presence,
>> and do not claim a place among his great men;

it is better for him to say to you, "Come up here,"

than for him to humiliate you before his nobles.

(Proverbs 25:6–7)

For all those who exalt themselves will be humbled,

and those who humble themselves will be exalted. (Luke

14:11)

When you humble yourself before the Lord and submit to his desires, he responds by entrusting you with greater influence. In the same way, when you walk humbly before pastors and church leaders, they are far more likely to grant you favor than if you are walking in pride. The principle is the same in each case. Avoid independence, and embrace submission and fellowship.

Greed

Jesus never promised us fame and fortune. The prosperity described in the Bible doesn't mean that your name will be on the bestseller list or that your music album will go platinum or that your painting will be hung at the Louvre Museum in Paris. Prosperity isn't about that.

True prosperity means that God will give you the measure of success you need in order to accomplish what he has commissioned you to do—all while demonstrating to the world that you are both dearly loved by him and truly in love with him. So if he needs you to be a spectacle to the nations of the magnificence of his resources, then he may indeed give you the wealth of Solomon. If he needs you to camp with the poor and rub elbows with the destitute of society, then he may allow you to be less distracted by finances—much like Jesus who had "no place to lay his head" (Luke 9:58).

In our human passion for luxury and comfort, we tend to crave outlandish wealth. We often engage in creativity, with money as a chief motivation. As singers, we want to make it big. As writers, we want a famous talk show host to promote our book to the masses. As architects, we want the biggest contracts and the most influential clients. As filmmakers, we want a worldwide blockbuster hit. Whatever your field of creativity, we can easily focus more on the dollar sign than the cross.

It is not bad to have money. But it is bad to serve money. When making a buck becomes your primary purpose for doing what you do, it is no longer worship. "You cannot serve both God and money" (Matthew 6:24).

Purity comes when we do what we do, whether or not there is financial compensation. For example, I love to write, I love to lead people in praise and worship, and I love to proclaim and demonstrate the gospel. I do these things for free on a daily basis as worship to the Lord. It's nice that I can be compensated for it now and then, but that's just a bonus. The focus is Christ. If I can devote myself to ministering to him, then he will provide for my needs. He will prosper me according to the mission he has for me.

I will not need to worry about what to eat, drink, or wear. (See Matthew 6:25–34.)

Check your own heart. If you find yourself serving the almighty dollar rather than Almighty God, the solution is not necessarily to stop being creative. Rather, the solution is to repent of greed. Put it on the cross through confession and a humble heart. Ask the Lord to help you see him clearly as more valuable than anything this world has to offer. Spend some time doing activities that won't earn money just to help you reset. Then keep God at the heart of your devotion and do everything as worship unto him. It's not wrong to be compensated for your work, but it is wrong to make compensation your chief motivation and purpose.

Selfishness

At the root of greed is selfishness. Selfishness is often expressed through fantasy. There is a difference between creativity and fantasy. Fantasy is about self-gratification whereas creativity is about giving. Fantasy puts unrealistic expectations on others whereas creativity invites others into a new experience. Fantasy points inward while creativity points outward.

When you engage your imagination, are you fantasizing or creating? Is it about you, or is it about serving God's purposes?

The difference between fantasy and creativity can be a fine line—the determining factor is typically the motivation behind what you do. For example, publicity isn't innately bad, but there is a difference between promoting yourself and trying to bless more people with a life-changing message. Likewise, personal expression isn't innately bad, but there is a difference between magnifying yourself and magnifying Christ in you. One is for your own benefit while the other is to benefit others. Even being recognized isn't innately bad, but there is a difference between stroking your own ego and truly giving God all the glory. In each case, one is fantasy, and the other is godly creativity.

One of the problems with fantasy is that by its very nature, it probably won't happen. (And if it does happen, it will only benefit self—a result completely contrary to the gospel.) Fantasy requires things of others that are usually centered on what we want to happen. Godly creativity, on the other hand, has a purpose rooted in what God wants to happen. Rather than requiring someone to respond or act a certain way for your benefit, righteous creativity invites the observer to respond a certain way for his or her own benefit.

When your imagination starts racing with ideas, pause for a moment and examine whether you're dealing in the realm of fantasy or creativity. Are you just dreaming up ways to puff yourself up, or are you worshipping Christ and influencing others for the better?

Apathy

When I was a teen, one of my youth pastors used to say that the opposite of love is not hate. Rather, he said, the opposite of love is apathy. When you hate someone, at least you're feeling something. But when you're apathetic, you feel nothing at all. Apathy causes us to simply stop caring. Apathy is the opposite of love.

It should make sense, then, that apathy would stand in opposition to empowered creativity. For one thing, we can't call it "limitless, love-filled creativity in action" if there is no love. How can we possibly have the right motivation if we don't care about others and how they might be affected or influenced by our work?

If God were apathetic toward mankind—if he simply didn't care—then there never would have been a mankind! If Noah had been apathetic, there never would have been an ark. If Moses had been apathetic, the Israelites might still be slaves in Egypt. If Jesus were apathetic, would he even have come in the first place? Would we even exist?

Apathy makes empowered creativity impossible. Apathy robs us of the most powerful motivation: love. Apathy keeps us from taking action—let alone being creative and innovative with that action.

If you truly want your creativity empowered, then you need to allow yourself to care. Ask the Lord to help you see people with his eyes. Ask him for compassion. Ask him for direction and motivation. Ask him for help with the worshipful project that's on your heart.

Empowered Creativity in Action

Dealing with the issues listed here can be a lifelong process. That's why grace is so important. Continually cry out to Jesus for freedom from all forms of sin. Ask the Holy Spirit to fill you with his presence and empower you to live like Jesus in word, thought, attitude, and deed. Ask God to give you divine inspiration for projects that you may not even be ready to handle.

Spend time in the presence of the Lord. The deeper you look into his heart, the more there is to discover. And the more you discover in God, the better you can express and reveal him.

Study his Word with the intent of engaging him on a personal level. Take time in prayer to dialogue with him. Listen to the truths that he has revealed to others.

Allow all these things to bring you into a clearer revelation of the heart of God, and then engage in the creative process to reveal him.

He will empower your creativity.

CONCLUSION

God didn't use the best writers to pen his Bible. He didn't use an expert shipbuilder to construct the ark. He didn't use the gifted craftsmen of Israel to make the bronze snake that brought healing to the people. And when Jesus called the disciples, he didn't select the best public speakers and the most qualified scholars. God simply called willing people who loved and revered him.

Are you willing? Will you choose to surrender your entire life—including your creativity—to the God who gave it all to you in the first place? Will you choose to pursue love no matter the cost?

These principles apply to all areas of creativity. As I mentioned in the beginning of this book, your particular expressions may be artistic in nature (painting, sculpting, dancing, singing, etc.), innovative in nature (inventing, planning, cooking, designing, etc.), or strategic in nature (business strategies, financial prowess, marketing ingenuity, etc.). Whatever the case, you now understand that God wants to use your creativity for kingdom purposes. He wants to partner with you to reveal his heart to the world.

Like King David, who purposed in his heart to build a temple for the Lord (even though God never asked for a temple), you have the liberty to run forward with creative expressions of worship. Whenever you engage in the creative process to glorify God, he will bless your work and even empower it for his intended purposes. Our Father loves to respond joyfully to the artwork of his children.

God isn't looking for virtuosos; he's looking for kids. In our world, talented adults tend to receive critiques and are never quite good enough. Kids, however, are met with an explosion of excitement for smearing some fingerpaint on a crinkled paper. You don't have to be the best writer, shipbuilder, craftsman, speaker, or scholar. All God is interested in is the heart of a child, wholly yielded to him. Set your affections on the Lord Jesus Christ, and he will respond by empowering your creativity.

Father, I commit to you every reader. I ask you to cultivate the seeds that have been planted within them through this book. Bind us all together as a mighty expression of your heart in this world—expressing your unfathomable presence in boundlessly unique ways. I ask you to come, Holy Spirit, and empower our creativity in Jesus's name. Amen.

ABOUT THE AUTHOR

Art Thomas is a missionary-evangelist who travels the world to train and equip Christians for Spirit-filled ministry. He is the president and CEO of *Wildfire Ministries International*—a global ministry that has spread the gospel to difficult regions, trained pastors, planted churches, and built a self-sustainable orphanage and primary school in rural Uganda.

Art is the producer and director of *Paid in Full*, a film that has trained tens of thousands to minister healing in Jesus's name, and *Voice of God*, a two-part film about hearing God's voice and prophetic ministry. He has authored several books, including *The Word of Knowledge in Action* and *Limitless Hope*.

Art now pastors at Roots Church, Assembly of God—a Spirit-filled network of house churches in Metro Detroit, Michigan, which began as a group of young adults in his living room.

Art and his wife, Robin, have two boys—Josiah and Jeremiah—and live in Romulus, Michigan.

For more information, please visit www.ArtThomas.org

www.ingramcontent.com/pod-product-compliance
Lightning Source LLC
Chambersburg PA
CBHW062059080426
42734CB00012B/2693